ROLE STRUCTURE AND ANALYSIS OF THE FAMILY

Volume 24, Sage Library of Social Research

Role Structure and Analysis of the Family

F. IVAN NYE

with Howard M. Bahr, Stephen J. Bahr,
John E. Carlson, Viktor Gecas,
Steven McLaughlin, and Walter L. Slocum

Volume 24
SAGE LIBRARY OF
SOCIAL RESEARCH

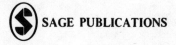 **SAGE PUBLICATIONS**   **Beverly Hills / London**

Copyright © 1976 by Sage Publications, Inc.

For information address:

SAGE PUBLICATIONS, INC.
275 South Beverly Drive
Beverly Hills, California 90212

SAGE PUBLICATIONS LTD
28 Banner Street
London EC1Y 8QE, England

Printed in the United States of America

Library of Congress Cataloging in Publication Data

Main entry under title:

Role structure and analysis of the family.

(Sage library of social research; v. 24)
1. Family—United States. 2. Family research—United States.
3. Social role. I. Nye, F. Ivan, 1918-   II. Title.
HQ536.R63   301.42′0973   75-40424
ISBN 0-8039-0663-3
ISBN 0-8039-0664-1 pbk.

THIRD PRINTING

CONTENTS

PREFACE

Obviously there are many ways that one can approach the description, analysis and explanation of family behavior. The psychoanalysts have focused on early childhood experience and the place of unconscious motivations as guides to adult family behavior. Structure-functionalists have tried to describe the interplay of the family with other social institutions, and under the leadership of Talcott Parsons, to extend that analysis into the role behavior of husbands, wives, and children within the family. Symbolic interactionists have focused on the meaning to the individual of decisions and behavior patterns of family members and those in meaningful interaction with family members. Recently, social exchange theorists have begun to reanalyze family behaviors in terms of rewards, costs, and goodness of outcomes. From these and more alternatives, why choose role analysis (and a rather special delineation of it at that) for structuring a program of research and theory development?

We believe that the role concept as developed in this volume has a number of advantages. Among these is its versatility. It can be profitably employed to describe the culture of a social institution and the groups which enact it. In this sense, it is a set of expectations for the behavior of occupants of all social positions—expectations based on a history of behaviors of innumerable occupants of these positions, not just the habits of a present position occupant. These expectations are incorporated in and form the substantive content of norms of the society. Too, the associated sanctions for enforcing role behavior are part of the culture. They may be written into laws and contracts to be enforced by special agencies or by informal, yet equally understood unwritten codes and equally effective institutionalized sanctions.

At the behavioral level, the concept finds expression in several constructs including role enactment, role-sharing (both among group members and among social organizations), role competence, role conflict, and role power. Thus, at the behavioral level, it is possible to determine whether a role is enacted by all or some fraction of position occupants. This can be an important issue in dealing with hypothesized roles—those emerging in the normative structure of the society or disappearing from it. Whether the role is part of only one or several positions, limited to a given social organization or part of more than one, can be determined. The level of competence of the role enactment can be estimated both by the role incumbent and by those with whom he or she interacts. Role conflict can be conceptually located within one or more roles; likewise, power can be usefully conceptualized and measured specific to each role domain.

Finally, the role concept can be utilized at the sociopsychological level, such as one's attachment to or identification with the role. Role activity disliked by many role occupants seems an especially likely target for social change, while those with which most occupants identify positively may persist indefinitely even though what would seem to be viable alternatives are readily available. Role strain may be predictive both of social change and of various outcomes for the individuals experiencing it.

Finally, the usefulness of a conceptual system to theory development and testing deserves mention. The role concept lends itself well to the assessment of rewards and costs which spouses provide one another. The two final chapters report our first exercises in utilizing role analysis to test and extend social exchange theory. Later papers will continue the application of this theoretical system, as well as symbolic interaction and perhaps others.

This volume reports the first major segment of a broad program of family research. It is, in effect, a large preliminary study in which the concepts are examined, reformulated at points, and empirically measured. How well these tasks have been accomplished may well be the principal contribution of the volume. However, data were collected from 210 couples randomly selected from lists of parents of third grade students. These data are reported here as the first available from the present role conceptualization and measurement. We are, of course, aware of limits on their adequacy for describing and analyzing American family roles. Larger samples from broader populations, refinements of indicators and more sophisticated data analysis procedures will be necessary for that task.

A sizable number of scholars have been involved in the initial stages of the program, from which this is the initial major report. Most of them appear as contributing authors and/or co-authors of chapters. All of the contributors were, at the time the project was planned, either faculty or doctoral candidates at Washington State University. In addition, we want to mention one or more sessions with major sociologists at other universities. These include Felix M. Berardo, Robert Bell, Glen Elder, Bernard Farber, David Kallen, and Murray Straus. Their ideas and reactions to ours helped shape the initial directions of the research. Cynthia Devary and Leigh Galloway made a presentable manuscript possible by their care in typing and checking the final draft.

Our debt to Washington State University is probably obvious, since it funded and supported the program under Project 2008 of the Agricultural Research Center. We appreciate that sizable support which made the research possible.

—F. Ivan Nye

Pullman, Washington
January 1976

PART I

PERSPECTIVE ON ROLES

Chapter 1

THE ROLE CONCEPT:
REVIEW AND DELINEATION

F. Ivan Nye and Viktor Gecas

Few sociological concepts are used more frequently than role—and its use is far from limited to sociology, with extensive use found in psychology, anthropology, social work, and other fields. Perhaps this is why no consensus has been reached on a specific meaning of the concept or the precise means of its measurement. In fact, most authors do not define it even for their own use, but permit the reader to sense a meaning from the way it is employed. This has led to a few major and many minor variations in its usage.

The importance, range, and diversity of the concept had reached a point by 1958 that Gross et al. (1958) devote five chapters to a review and formulation of the concept prior to applying it to their study of the role of superintendent. In their 1966 review, Biddle and Thomas listed 343 articles and books relating to role theory. This represented a growth from 25 in 1938 and from 112 in 1950. However, after reaching 278 in 1956, the increase in role literature showed signs of leveling off, but growth had not ceased by the last year of the above survey.

Along with Gross et al.'s (1958) and Biddle and Thomas' (1966) extensive and systematic reviews, a number of other book-length treatments of the role concept and its uses have recently appeared: Banton (1965), from an anthropological perspective, stresses the historical and cross-cultural development of the concept; Heiss (1968) emphasizes the expression of role theory in the family sociology literature; Znaniecki (1965) discusses roles from a symbolic interactionist perspective; and Jackson (1972) offers a collection of essays focusing on the utility of the role concept in sociological theory.

Besides these major comprehensive reviews of the concept, a number of review articles have dealt with special problems in its development and use. Such comprehensive treatments will not be attempted here. Rather, we will focus on some of the key issues that have appeared in conceptualizing the role concept. The reader is referred to the above as competent and relatively full reviews of the concept.

ROLES AS CULTURAL PRESCRIPTIONS VERSUS BEHAVIORAL REGULARITIES

There are at least two distinct traditions within sociology re-garding the concept of role: the structural tradition initiated by Ralph Linton (1936, 1945); and the interactionist tradition, gain-ing its coherence and impetus from the social psychology of George H. Mead (1934). Briefly, the difference between these two orientations is one of emphasis. The structuralists define role as an element of culture (normative) associated with a given social status or position. In Linton's (1936: 114) words:

A role represents the dynamic aspect of a status. The individual is socially assigned to a status and occupies it with relation to other statuses. When he puts the rights and duties which constitute the status into effect, he is performing a role.

In his later work (1945: 77), Linton more pointedly stressed the cultural context of roles:

Role will be used to designate the sum total of the culture patterns associated with a particular status. It thus includes the attitudes, values, and behavior ascribed by the society to any and all persons occupying the status.

The interactionist tradition, on the other hand, lays major emphasis on the *emergent* quality of roles—that is, a conception of roles as behavioral regularities emerging out of social interaction. For example, for Turner (1962: 25), "Role refers to a pattern which can be regarded as the consistent behavior of a single type of actor." Because of this greater emphasis on the behavioral expression of roles, the interactionist perspective is more likely to stress the processual, developmental, and even creative aspects of role behavior. Derivative concepts such as role-playing and role-taking, stressing the developmental aspects of role interaction, occupy a more prominent place in this orientation than in the structuralist view of roles.

The emphasis on the emergence of roles from social interaction is carried perhaps farthest by Turner. In his recent book *Family Interaction* (1970), Turner applies the concept of role to such social categories as "antagonist" or "dissenter" (1970: 186). It is not evident that there are cultural expectations concerning the proper or necessary behavior of one in a position of antagonist or dissenter, nor are the positions of antagonist or dissenter part of the culture of a society.[1] Rather, people in various positions, such as member of a small group, enact their roles differently from others—some dissent more, some harmonize more, etc. These behavioral regularities may, of course, result in behavioral expectations of the participants in the social group. But there is no reason to expect that they would go beyond the expectations of the group members. What seems to have occurred in small group research is that a position is inferred from a type of distinctive behavior. This reverses the structuralist process of expecting certain behavior from persons occupying positions—positions are inferred from descriptive types of behavior.

This use of the role concept may be futher illuminated by reviewing a list of roles which occur in Turner's extensive discussion of family roles. A few can reasonably be derived from culturally defined positions. Thus, cooking, housekeeping, and child care roles usually are associated with the position wife and/or mother. Female, aged, and child roles correspond to the position of female, aged person, or child. However, a much larger aggregate of roles is not derivable from any culturally defined position. These include from Turner's work: encourager, harmonizer, compromiser, aggressor, blocker, recognition seeker, mediator, antagonist, dissenter, irresponsible critic, advocate, challenger, hero, tyrannical, submissive, and authoritarian (1970: 185-216). (From a stucturalist perspective, these designations would be more descriptive of *styles* of behavior rather than of roles in their own right.)

The difference between the structural and interactionist positions on role is not only a difference in emphasis (prescriptions versus behavior), but also a difference in the types of social contexts considered for role analysis. The structuralist view is most appropriate to the study of roles in *formal* organizations or groups, where the cultural definitions for the roles are fairly clear. Interactionists, on the other hand, are more comfortable with analyses of roles in relatively unstructured, informal groups, where roles are vaguely defined and where there is a good deal of latitude in role behavior. The family, of course, is an advantageous context for the study of roles since it has strong elements of both formal structure and informal interaction.

Most, but not all, scholars appear to be aware of both basic elements of the role phenomenon: a set of expectations which is part of the culture and typical behavior of persons occupying a status (position) which, in fact, either validates the cultural expectations or emerges to create new roles. Sociologists who are more interested in social structure find the cultural emphasis more congenial while social psychologists, with their focus on behavior, have employed the behavioral definition. Gross et al. succinctly sum up an important aspect of the controversy in these words:

> Another reason for some of the differences in definition is simply semantic; the same phenomena are frequently given different names. Thus, what Linton and Newcomb define as a role, Davis defines as a status. What Davis defines as a role, Newcomb calls role behavior and Sarbin role enactment [Gross et al., 1958: 17].

It would be possible to resolve the conflicting definitions by assigning the single term "role" to a set of cultural expectations of behavior, attitudes, and values, while employing dynamic concepts such as role enactment, role performance, or role behavior to the actual behavior performed in enacting the role. While any individual scholar is likely to be more interested in one or the other, awareness of the other and some common role language would greatly increase the value of the concept.

Our study orients more to the structural properties of roles. Until now, at least, the family has been characterized by a relatively high degree of normative structure. Certain duties and privileges have been prescribed for husbands, wives, mothers, fathers, and to some extent children, and many activities have been proscribed to all or some family members. While this structure has become less rigid recently, still the normative prescriptions and proscriptions are relatively well defined in comparison with many other groups, and especially compared to groups of subjects assembled to solve problems in small group experiments.

We suggest, therefore, that the cultural content, the normative prescriptions and proscriptions, have relatively large influence on the behavior of husbands, wives, fathers, mothers, and children and, therefore, it is important in describing and explaning *family* behavior that these cultural guides to role behavior be measured and analyzed. Consequently, our further elaboration of the role concept will proceed from the structuralist perspective. This is not to ignore or deprecate the significance of role behavior, which does not necessarily correspond to the norms. Major components of the study will involve the measurement of role enactment and of the sanctions employed to enforce role prescriptions and proscriptions. The latter is important in distinguishing between prescriptions (which are enforced) and mere preferences for one rather than another behavior.

POSITION AS HAVING ONE ROLE VERSUS MANY

In relation to a given position, role has been employed both in the singular and plural; for example, the *role* of mother or the *roles* of a mother. Linton employed the singular, gathering all the expected behavior of position into one role. While he speaks of the roles of an individual, he has reference to the fact that each person occupies several positions, each of which involves one role. As a consequence, each person enacts several roles but only by virtue of occupying a number of positions (Linton, 1936: 114).

In contrast, Merton, Gross, et al., and Bates argue that each position includes a number of roles. Merton (1957: 3) writes:

> A particular social status involves, not a single associated role, but an array of associated roles. This is a basic characteristic of social structure. This fact of structure can be registered by a distinctive term, role-set, by which I mean that *complement of role relationships which persons have by virtue of occupying a particular social status.*

Merton offers an example in the status of public school teacher, which has its distinctive role-sets, relating the teacher to pupils, colleagues, the school principal and superintendent, the Board of Education, professional organizations of teachers, and Parent Teachers Associations. Two important points are made above: that a position typically includes more than one role, and that roles are established on the basis of people occupying other relevant positions. In this formulation, it is not the duties per se that are involved directly but services to other categories of people occupying other statuses.

Gross et al. (1958) take a similar but not identical position. They view the role as composed of a number of *segments*, each of which is a set of expected behaviors which a relevant group holds for the role incumbent. "A role sector is defined as a set of expectations applied to the relationship of a focal position to a single counter position," (Gross et al., 1958: 60). For example, a school board member holds a set of expectations concerning the behavior of the superintendent, teachers hold another, city officials another, etc. Each of these sectors of expectations are considered role sectors. Actually, they avoid direct use of the plural in dealing with roles, but in emphasizing the different bundles of responsibilities included in the overall role, they point to the necessity of breaking the global concept of role down into more homogeneous sets of expectations. Use of the concept role-sector corresponds with Merton's role-set, and both break the global concept *role* down into more manageable subunits.

Bates (1956) is even more specific in attributing plural roles to any one position. He defines role as part, but only part, of a position. Inspecting the postion of father, he delimits such roles as provider, disciplinarian, playmate, etc. Even more explicitly than Merton or Gross, he opts for a number of roles in each position.

Whether a majority of role scholars view role in the singular, composed of many more specific activities without internal organization, or whether they see it as multiple roles associated with a single position is unknown. It may be that casual reference to role is less likely to differentiate among the expectation subunits and therefore refer to such global uses of the concept as "the female role" or the "role of the Black," whereas the theorist or researcher who must subject the concept to close scrutiny and attempt to describe it more concretely may feel the need to break the global concept into more homogeneous subunits and be more likely to view the behavioral expectations of a status in the plural.

Furthermore, to utilize role in the singular, as did Linton, may be more useful in simple, static societies than in dynamic, complex ones. Provided one knows the age of a person, in the former societies it might communicate quite well to refer to the role of the female. A female of thirty years of age would be married, have children and be engaged in specified tasks well segregated from male role behavior. However, in current Western industrial societies she may be single, married with no children, married with children, or unmarried with children. She may or may not be considerably engaged in housekeeper activities. Therefore, if only the position is specified—and especially if it is a general one such as a sexual position—little can be assumed about the role behavior connected to it. Presumably this is why Merton, Gross et al., and Bates have elected to break this global category of role down into the more specific, concrete sets of expectations which they term role sectors, role sets, and simply roles, respectively.

ROLE SETS, ROLE SECTORS, AND ROLE CLUSTERS

While the Merton, Gross et al., and Bates role formulations are similar in that each divides the global concept into more homogeneous units, the differences are considerable. Merton and Gross et al. coincide in choosing other positions as the basis of subdivision. The rationale for this is that there are different sets of expectations existing on the part of the categories of people served by occupants of the position. Thus, a sector of the role of superintendent is composed of the expectations of school board members, another of teachers, another of parents, town officials, etc. Merton's "role set" is made up of the different expectations of the set of people the superintendent serves. Bates' roles, in contrast, are composed of a homogeneous set of norms. More specifically, "[A] role [is] part of a social position consisting of a more or less integrated or related sub-set of social norms which is distinguishable from other sets of norms forming the same position" (Bates, 1956: 314). These clusters of norms make up clusters of roles which constitute a social position. Thus, Bates, drawing illustrations from the family, delineates such roles as sex partner, housekeeper, teacher, and disciplinarian. He does not specify the special categories of people served in each role. The tasks form the basis of the subdivision of the concept, rather than categories of people. For example, in the housekeeper role, the mother serves equally her husband, her sons and daughters, and even an aged parent, if one is living in the home.

If the Bates model were applied to he role of the superintendent, then, instead of role sectors or role set, one would find a role of financial officer of the system, a personnel role for hiring, dismissing and supervising faculty, a public relations role, and possibly a disciplinary role for children. If the Merton or Gross et al. model were applied to the family, the father would have a role set made up of the positions of mother, son, daughter, kinfolk, and perhaps teacher and PTA, or role sectors of expectations from each of them. The basis for subdividing his role would not be a set of duties which he would render to one, two, or several categories of individuals, such as housekeeper, socializer of child, and the like, but the expectations of wives, sons, daughters, teachers, and the like.

Bates also proposes that, although a position is composed of a number of roles, *the same role can be found in more than one position*. For example, the child socialization role is part of the positions of both father and mother. Furthermore, the role is also part of the positions of school teacher, Boy Scout leader, and leader of a youth group in the church. Thus, Bates argues that, although roles are parts of positions, they are not limited to a single position. This characteristic of the concept adds complexity but also a desirable flexibility, since some role responsibilities are shared between father and mother or between spouses, and some between family members and occupants of positions in other social organizations such as schools, day care personnel, and leaders of children's organizations. This flexibility maximizes the usefulness of the concept for studying social change both within and between social organizations.

SUBCULTURAL UNIFORMITIES AND VARIATIONS IN ROLE DEFINITIONS

Since role is a cultural concept, any group may normatively define and enforce role definitions. But, in a heterogeneous society, a role may be normatively defined in some subcultures and not in others. Likewise, it is reasonable to anticipate that specific families also develop distinctive norms (Nye and MacDougal, 1958), and even within specific families, the husband may hold one set of normative definitions about appropriate family roles while the wife holds another set. Thus, role norms, sanctions, and enactment may vary, in principle, from being supported by everyone to only a few in a society or some social unit within it. The degree of support Jackson (1966) calls "role crystalization." A role affirmed by all or nearly all respondents is viewed as fully crystalized.

EMERGING AND DISAPPEARING ROLES

Along with subcultural variations, we can also expect variations over time within identifiable social units. The family literature suggests that some new roles associated with parental and conjugal positions are emerging, while others may be declining. For example, Hacker (1957) has written of a new sexual role for men in an article titled "New Burdens of Masculinity." Rainwater has demonstrated the presence of the idea of duty in the sexual behavior of Protestant men above the lower-class level (Rainwater, 1965: 104). In that segment, eighty-five percent expressed concern for the wife's sexual enjoyment while only thirty-seven percent of lower-lower-class husbands did so. In what may be termed "emergent roles," a role may be perceived by a majority of adults in one sector but not in others in the society. On the other hand, there is wome evidence of declining support for the norms of the kinship and housekeeper roles, even though historically they have been crystalized roles.

The procedure developed to test for the presence of a role in the normative structure is to ask a sample of respondents (1) whether it is a spouse's duty to engage in the role behavior, and (2) whether, if the position occupant does not enact the role, he or she would be subjected to sanctions. If a majority respond affirmatively to both questions, the role exists in a normative sense for the population sampled. However, it is possible to more than dichotomize roles as present or not present by utilizing Jackson's concept of crystalization and characterizing roles as relatively more or less fully crystalized (Jackson, 1966).

DELINEATION OF FAMILY ROLES

Our use of the role concept draws first from Linton in *The Cultural Background of Personality:* "*Role* will be used to designate the sum total of the culture patterns associated with a particular status. It thus includes the attitudes, values and behavior ascribed by the society to any and all persons occupying this status," (Linton, 1945: 77). To the basic idea of a role as a set of cultural expectations is added a refinement implied by Gross et al. and specified by Merton and by Bates—that the behavioral expectations attached to a role are too numerous and diverse to be subsumed under a single concept. Therefore, the concept is more effective if it is used in the plural. For each position, there are a number of roles, each of which is composed of a related, more or less homogeneous set of behaviors normatively prescribed and proscribed, expected of those who occupy a given status. This delineation follows Bates more closely than Merton in that it is based on the similarity of a bundle of behaviors rather than on another status to which these behaviors are related. Therefore maternal roles are identified as housekeeping or recreation rather than roles related to oldest daughter, youngest son, and the like. The principle of parsimony suggests that as few roles as possible be delineated provided that each role does not include unduly diverse behaviors. The larger the number of roles delineated for any given position, the more specific and homogeneous can be the content of the role. Therefore, the criteria of parsimony and homogeneity are necessarily in conflict, and there is no objective basis for resolving such conflict.

After a review of family literature, eight roles in the positions of spouse, parent, or both were identified. These are: provider, housekeeper, child care, child socialization, sexual, recreational, therapeutic, and kinship. Traditionally, housekeeper, child care, and sexual roles have been assigned by the norms to the wife, with provider assigned to the husband, and kinship and child socialization roles to both. However, there has been a tendency in recent years for wives to share enactment of the provider and husbands the housekeeper and child care roles. Thus, part of the research task is to determine to what extent spouses feel that roles should be shared and to what extent they are, in practice, shared—both between spouses and between the family and other social organizations.

The therapeutic and recreational roles and a male sexual role are viewed as changing from permissive to prescriptive activity; that is, one might in the past, if he (she) felt in a helpful mood, listen to one's spouse's problems or might choose not to do so without feeling remiss in one's duty. But it is hypothesized that currently spouses see therapeutic assistance not as permissive but as a duty to help one's spouse (Nye, 1974). The same is hypothesized of the recreational and the husband's enactment of the sexual role; that is, becoming crystalized.

The reverse process of role "decrystalization" may be equally important—the degree to which role responsibilities which were formerly required of position occupants are currently no more than preferred or optional behavior. The latter process is hypothesized to be occurring with respect to the housekeeper and kinship roles. Data bearing on this issue are presented in Chapters 4 and 5.

DIMENSIONS OF ROLE ANALYSIS

The role concept has provided such a fertile ground for social scientists that it has spawned a number of derivative concepts providing various dimensions of analysis. We will focus on several of these in our assessment of family roles. Along with the normative dimension (what *should* be done or who should do it) and the behavior dimension (what *is* done who *does* it, and *how* it is done), we will also consider the degree to which individuals are committed to the roles (role commitment), the evaluation of their own and their spouse's role performances (role competence), the extent to which they worry about their role performance (role strain), the amount of conflict which occurs over these roles (role conflict), and the outcome of role conflict (role power).

NOTE

1. This is not to deny that there are some positions or occupations in our society which have, as part of their role expectations, the occupant criticize, dissent, oppose, or mediate. Some examples which come to mind include the literary critic, the mediator in labor-management disputes, the politician whose party is the "loyal opposition," and the linebacker on a football team.

Chapter 2

ROLE CONSTRUCTS: MEASUREMENT

F. Ivan Nye

Chapter 1 briefly reviewed the concept of role and developed a delineation of it. The present chapter has the purposes of (1) listing and briefly describing a number of concepts developed from the basic role concept; (2) indicating their usefulness for family research; and (3) describing the empirical indicators which have been developed for each. Granted that each might well be the subject of a chapter in its own right, space limitations and other considerations have led to no more than a brief treatment in the present manuscript.

NORMATIVE DIMENSIONS

In Chapter 1, we outlined a delineation of the role concept as a set of norms—a part of the culture—which prescribes and pro-scribes behavior to occupants of one or more positions. However, as we noted there, not all family roles are "equally normative." As Jackson (1966) and others have noted, some roles are more fully "crystalized" in the normative structure than others and, as we stated in Chapter 1, some are hypothesized to exist and cannot be taken for granted. Therefore, different items seemed to be needed for traditional roles which everyone, or virtually everyone, would take for granted and for those which there is some basis for thinking are emerging from optional to prescribed or proscribed behaviors, or moving *out* of the normative structure back to optional behavior. Our procedure was different for the two categories of roles. We *assumed* the existence of child care, child socialization, provider, and housekeeper roles. We *hypothesized* the existence of therapeutic, recreational, male sexual, and kinship roles. Taking this into account, we regarded it as a waste of the respondent's time to ask if a duty existed to care for or socialize children, earn the economic support of the family or enact the housekeeper role. Therefore, we asked only whose duty it is to enact the role and whether it is a sole or a shared responsibility. Illustrative of the measurement of this category of traditional roles is the normative item for the housekeeper role:

Who do you feel should do the housekeeping?

  (1) husband entirely
  (2) husband more than the wife
  (3) husband and wife exactly the same
  (4) wife more than the husband
  (5) wife entirely
  (6) other (comment) _____

The same format was employed for the child care, child socialization, and provider roles.

For the less obvious roles—therapeutic, recreational, sexual, and kinship—the respondent was given an option of saying that it was not the duty of anyone. The wording varied slightly because of the differing possibilities for sharing the role. The maximum choice was offered for the recreational role, worded as follows:

In your opinion, whose duty is it to organize and start family recreation?

  (1) husband entirely
  (2) husband more than wife
  (3) husband and wife exactly the same
  (4) optional—it doesn't matter who does it provided it is
        done
  (5) wife more than husband
  (6) wife entirely
  (7) it is no one's duty

Another variant in asking the normative question was used for the therapeutic role:

Some people feel that it is not part of a wife's duty to help her husband with his personal problems; others feel it is a duty. What are your feelings? (Same question for husband.)

    (1)   she should do it
    (2)   it is preferable she do it
    (3)   it is optional for her
    (4)   she shouldn't do it

SANCTIONS TO ENFORCE NORMS

The norm that someone should perform or refrain from a set of acts can be interpreted in several ways, varying from an idealized pattern (which no one really expects will occur) to mere preferences that one type is better than another. We opted for prescriptions and proscriptions realistic enough so that they represent possible and feasible behavior patterns, and, as such, behavior can and usually does conform to the norms. The test applied to this model is whether negative sanctions are forthcoming for nonperformance of the role. Sanctions provide evidence that the society (or the relevant segment of it) regards the role as sufficiently important and conformity to it possible to most position occupants so that conformity to the norms should and is enforced. Jackson (1966) refers to this dimension as "intensity."

In the traditional and obvious roles (housekeeper, provider, child care, and child socialization), sanctions were worded in terms of actions (ostracism) against persistent nonconformers. For example, in the child socialization role, the question was posed:

If a woman didn't teach her children the things they need to know in order to be able to take care of themselves and in order to get along with others, how would you feel toward her and her family? (Circle all answers that fit your feelings.)

    (1)   I would not choose them as close friends
    (2)   would not want my children to play with their children
    (3)   would not want to be in the same social group
    (4)   would not want to talk with them often

(5) would not want them in the same neighborhood
(6) it would not make any difference to me

These items are intended to measure the presence and severity of the ostracism one who violated the norms of the role would encounter. The most severe would be to exclude them from living in the community.

In the "emerging" or less obvious roles, such strong sanctions seemed inappropriate. For example, it seemed unlikely that anyone would not choose a person as a friend because that person failed to perform a therapeutic role for his (her) spouse. For this reason, disapproval was utilized as the form of sanction instead of ostracism. Respondents were asked whether they would strongly disapprove, disapprove, be unconcerned with, or even actually approve a spouse's failure to enact the role. With respect to one role, the provider, respondents were asked both types of sanction questions. Comparing the two, it is evident that the ostracism measure is a much stronger sanction. Almost every respondent disapproved of a husband who didn't make an effort to support his family, but not all would ostracize him (see Table 9.2).

It may be evident from the above that both the norms of the roles and the sanctions to enforce them are variables rather than discrete entities. In a population, every member of the society or subunit of it *might* agree that a role exists (in the normative sense, applied here), but this is not necessarily true. Near consensus does exist with respect to the provider and socialization roles for fathers, and child care and socialization roles for mothers, but, as later chapters will show, large proportions of the population also ascribe responsibilities in the housekeeper and child care roles to the husband as well as to the wife. There is far from unanimity in the sample with respect to therapeutic, recreational, and kinship roles, although a majority subscribe to each of these. The same is true of sanctions. The proportion who would support each type of sanctions varies from role to role, and nowhere is there complete unanimity. Since incomplete and varying approximations of consensus exist, some standard must be selected for deciding that a role exists. If a majority of the sample from a population affirms the existence of a role and would negatively sanction nonperformance, then such a role is assumed to exist in that population at the time the data were gathered. This is the same standard as that employed by Jackson (1966).

This way of conceptualizing and measuring norms provides for *degrees* of consensus with respect to roles and variations on consensus and strength of sanctions employed. We shall see later, in Chapter 9, called "The Comparative Analysis of Roles," that such conceptualization and measurement permits comparison *among* roles with respect to degree of consensus concerning both norms and sanctions.

NORMATIVE ROLE SHARING

Hardly less important than the existence of a role is who or how many different position occupants ought to enact it. In a society with a sharply segregated role structure, there may be a minimum of normative role-sharing, but differentiated, technologically advanced societies, at least, appear to be characterized by extensive role-sharing. For example, we have noted that the child socialization role is normatively shared by the father, mother, school teacher, minister, and youth leader.

Especially during a period of changes in role enactment and the advocacy of even greater changes in sex role enactment, this normative dimension of role is of widespread interest. Since we shall see later that there is no necessary correspondence among the normative, enactment, and power dimensions of role, one might expect that the size of these discrepancies is predictive of marital satisfaction, marital instability, and/or other group and personal outcomes. Likewise, it can pose such questions as how the norms of sharing one role are affected by sharing in another—for example, how the full-time employment of the wife affects the norms of performing the housekeeper role. Role-sharing indicators have been described above.

ROLE ENACTMENT

The actual role behavior of actors in the relevant positions is not necessarily identical with the norms for their roles and is separable from them. Therefore, a measure of role enactment was also constructed. Again, two types of items were necessary because some roles are performed by spouses primarily for and by each other, while others are performed for third persons and sometimes *by* third persons as well as for each spouse. Representative of the first is the item measuring enactment of the therapeutic role:

If you have a problem that bothers you and you tell your husband, does he: (circle as many as are correct)

(1) usually listen without doing anything about it
(2) usually sympathize
(3) usually prefer not to be bothered by your problems
(4) usually criticize you for having the problem
(5) usually try to help solve your problems
(6) give reassurance and affection

Although the therapeutic role is important to adults, survival does not, apparently, depend on its enactment within the family group or even by anyone. Therefore, it should be assumed that not all spouses will enact it and similar roles. (We regard responses 3 and 4 above as refusals to enact the role.)

Within the present role framework, two measures of role enactment are potentially important: (1) the division of labor between spouses and (2) the division between them and other role enactors—either within the family or in other social organizations. In the present research, principal emphasis has been placed on the first of these, sharing of role enactment between the spouses. Below is a sample item from the child care role:

Who takes care of the physical needs of your children?

(1) husband entirely
(2) husband more than wife
(3) husband and wife exactly the same
(4) wife more than husband
(5) wife entirely
(6) other (comment) _____ _____

This role delineation permits role enactment by other family members or by hired help or personnel of other organizations. While this is a potentially important aspect of role enactment, it is given only limited attention in the present study. We did ask whether others helped with child care, socialization, housekeeper, provider, and therapeutic roles.

A FURTHER NOTE ON ROLE SHARING

At the risk of being repetitious, we want to emphasize the distinction made earlier between role as a unit of culture—a set of duties and responsibilities prescribed for occupants of a position (such as mother or father)—and role enactment, role conflict, and other behavioral concepts. Role sharing may be at either the cultural or behavioral level. For example, many mothers share in the enactment of a provider role, but this does not necessarily mean that they have a duty to do so or that negative sanctions would be forthcoming if they do not enter the labor force. To use another example, men have always participated in sexual intercourse, but it appears that a duty and generalized expectation that they would provide for the sexual gratification of their partners is only now crystalizing and becoming a normative element in the culture.

ROLE COMPETENCE

An important additional component of role enactment is how *well* a role is performed. This is an important concept to a number of theoretical perspectives but is perhaps most relevent to social exchange theory. Those who are competent in performing roles provide more rewards for group members than those who are not. Actually, competence can be anchored at the negative end of the dimension by role refusal or other types of nonperformance.

There are two reference groups available to the respondent in evaluating his or her own role competence and that of the spouse. These are (1) the society as a whole and (2) working associates and neighbors. These may lead to quite different evaluations of and feelings about competence. In the present research, the reference group was left up to the respondent to use a comparison in ranking self and spouse. For example, men were asked this question about the provider role:

Men vary a good deal in ability to provide for a family. Would you estimate that you are:

(1) an exceptionally good provider
(2) better than average provider
(3) about an average provider
(4) somewhat less than average provider
(5) not a very good provider
(6) not able or can't find work

The above type of item was employed for all except the sexual role. It was believed that spouses would have too little information concerning the sexual role enactment of other spouses to realistically evaluate themselves or their spouses. In another study, we have tried to develop an indicator of sexual competence.

While the concept and measurement of role competence was developed with the special intent to utilize it as a means of measuring rewards, its potential utility is considerably wider. For example, it can be used to predict and explain role-sharing, with the person more competent in the role more likely to perform it, or in the study of family power (still within the exchange framework) more power accorded to effective role enactor.

ROLE IDENTIFICATION

There are a number of reasons for conceptualizing and measuring role identification, including it as an end in itself, comparable with studies of marital or job satisfaction. Or it might be employed as an independent variable—to predict marital satisfaction, for example. Our special interest in it relates to social change, both in role-sharing between spouses and especially to the possibility that a given role will cease or largely cease to be enacted within the family and be largely or entirely enacted by persons in social organizations other than the family. For example, a finding that few women identify with the housekeeper role would lead to the expectation that the trend for more meals to be prepared and eaten in restaurants rather than homes is likely to continue at a rapid rate (Chapter 5). Or does the strong identification of parents with the child care and/or socialization roles suggest that the change to day care center care of children may be less precipitous than might otherwise be expected (Chapter 3)?

Identification, as presently measured, probably is multidimensional, including (1) intrinsic satisfaction or dissatisfaction directly associated with performing the activities of the role, (2) feeling (or lack of feeling) that performance of the role is essential for occupying the position of spouse or parent, and (3) positive or negative feelings about bringing an alternative role enactor into the patterns of familial interaction to enact the role.

The question devised to measure role identification asked if the role occupant would want to delegate or share the responsibility for the role if a reasonable alternative were available. For example, with respect to the housekeeper role, the question was worded:

Suppose you had a very large income for life, making it possible for you to hire a well-trained competent person to help you with the above tasks. Do you think you would do so?

(1) I certainly would
(2) I probably would
(3) I might
(4) I probably wouldn't
(5) I certainly wouldn't

We believe, in retrospect, that the wording of this item leads to an overestimate of role identification, since it implies the presence of an unrelated person enacting a role within the social space of the family. Probably many would not welcome the presence of an unrelated person, whatever his or her skills and usefulness.

ROLE STRAIN

We have thought of role strain primarily as a dependent variable, indicative of problems in role enactment for the role player. However, since strain is a cost, it could be used as one predictor of marital dissatisfaction or marital dissolution. Also, in other research settings, it might be useful to utilize it as a predictor of mental illness.

We think of strain in terms of such mental states as worry,

anxiety, or guilt. Presumably these are interrelated but not inter-changeable mental states. We chose to utilize the degree of worry as the empirical indicator. A sample item reads as follows:

All things considered, how do you feel about the way you keep house?

    (1)   I worry frequently because I wish I could do better
    (2)   I worry once in a while about the way I keep house
    (3)   I don't think much about it one way or the other
    (4)   I usually feel that I have done a good job
    (5)   I am satisfied completely with the way I keep house

CONFLICT IN ROLES

A considerable literature exists on role conflict. As Gross et al. (1958) suggest, this is usually conceptualized as interrole conflict in which the norms or behavior patterns of one role are incon-sistent with those of a second role of the actor. It has also been used to refer to intrarole strain in which two or more categories of people hold conflicting expectations concerning the behavior appropriate to a single role. Neither of these usages was excluded from the present conceptualization of conflict in roles. However, additional sources of conflict in roles may be identified. Lack of role enactment may be one. For example, present data show that about thirty percent of husbands and half that proportion of wives refuse to enact the therapeutic role or do so in ways apparently more hurtful than helpful. Others disagree on how a role should be shared or who has the responsibility for making role decisions. Or the level of role competence may be so low that role conflict develops about it. At the widest level of definition, these could all be subsumed under the heading of intrarole conflict, but en-compass considerably more than that term has usually included.

As presently measured, conflict in roles includes conflict at the overt level. For example, the following item was used to measure conflict in the recreational role:

How frequently, if ever, do you and your wife openly dis-agree or argue concerning recreation?

(1)   very frequently
(2)   frequently
(3)   sometimes
(4)   seldom
(5)   never

This appears to be a good indicator for overt conflict; however, if one wishes to include conflicting positions of spouses, whether or not these are expressed overtly, then it is too limited. Levinger found in a study of couples seeking divorce (1966) that much disliked behavior of a spouse never results in overt conflict. Therefore, this indicator does not measure all role conflict, in the more comprehensive sense. We suggest later that this limitation on the indicator of conflict is probably largely responsible for some of the differences in role conflict reported by wives and husbands.

ROLE POWER

The measure of role power was developed with the hope of improving on earlier conjugal power instruments. The widely used Blood and Wolfe (1960) instrument has been criticized as not specifying overt disagreement. And although it and some other instruments included a considerable variety of items, they were not role-specific. The present measure takes both of these problems into account in focusing on contested disagreements specific to each role. It provides single-item indicators or power in each role and permits the construction of indices from two up to six roles. (No power measures were devised for the sexual, or therapeutic roles. Power measures in these latter roles would be more difficult to devise and perhaps more difficult to defend conceptually.) The form of the power indicator is illustrated from the recreational role:

If there is a disagreement concerning recreation, who makes the final decision?

(1)   husband always
(2)   husband more often than wife
(3)   husband and wife exactly the same

(4)   wife more often than husband
(5)   wife always
(6)   absolutely no disagreement on this role

This indicator has the advantages discussed above, but it has the limitation already discussed that not all disagreements reach the verbal stage. Some are conceded by a spouse because he or she knows the attitude of the other and prefers conceding the issue to the alternative of engaging in a contest with the spouse.

We find role power interesting for the internal analysis of role phenomenon. We asked who should perform each role, who does perform it, how frequent the disagreement with respect to it, and finally who makes the decisions when disagreements occur. It seems plausible that the person who, normatively, has responsibility for the role, enacts, and that the one who enacts it makes decisions with respect to the role if a difference of opinion occurs.

THE SAMPLE

This program of role research envisions a series of projects, of which the present one is the first. It was designed to be a testing ground for the conceptualization and measurement of role properties, yet it was hoped that such conceptualization and measurement were sufficiently advanced to provide worthwhile substantive findings.

With these objectives in mind, a medium-sized Washington county (Yakima) was selected for the inital research. It is an unusually diverse county, including one small metropolitan area centering in the city of Yakima. It contains a sizable farm population (eleven percent) and one of the larger Native American and Mexican-American concentrations in the state of Washington. The education level, according to both the 1960 and 1970 censuses, was close to the state average. The income level was slightly below the state average in 1960, a difference which was to increase by 1970. While no one county can be defended as "representative" of the state, Yakima seemed to provide more diversity of population than would be true of any other county.

The study of family roles is not limited to any one segment of the family life cycle, but for the initial study it was decided to focus it upon parents of children of school and preschool age. Parents of children in grade three were selected as the initial population, and a random sample was drawn from parents of children in that grade in the public and parochial schools of the county. The sample was limited to families with two parents present, including in some families a stepparent.

Parallel questionnaires were designed for husband and wife. Most items were identical except that "your wife" or "your husband" was used as appropriate to refer to the spouse. Some social background items which seemed to represent needless duplication were eliminated from the husband's questionnaire. Serial numbers linked the husband's and wife's questionnaires so that any item in either instrument could be analyzed in relationship to any item in the spouse's questionnaire.

Both instruments contained the series of role items described above and the usual social background variables. In addition, certain items were added for two dissertations (Bahr, 1972; Carlson, 1972), the Blood and Wolfe (1960) items measuring conjugal power and a more detailed description of recreational preferences and practices. These inclusions resulted in a long instrument of nineteen pages—overlong for obtaining a high return but needed for the purposes of the initial study.

After three follow-up letters, the return was forty-six percent from at least one spouse, netting a return of 210 couples in which a usable questionnaire was received from both husband and wife. Since data were obtained in the summer of 1970, they were comparable with those obtained in the U.S. Census of 1970. Roughly comparable data are available for the state of Washington and the United States (U.S. Bureau of the Census, 1972) and limited data are available for Yakima County in the City and County Data Book for 1972.

The sample more closely approximates the state of Washington than it does the United States (Table 2.1). For education completed, the sample corresponds very closely to the state. The sample includes a substantially larger proportion of couples with incomes under $10,000 (forty-two compared to twenty-nine for Washington and thirty-five percent for the United States). This difference reflects the substantially lower income in the county in

Table 2.1

COMPARISONS OF THE SAMPLE WITH CENSUS INFORMATION
ON SELECT CHARACTERISTICS OF ADULT MALES (AGE 35-44)
FOR THE STATE OF WASHINGTON AND TOTAL UNITED STATES

	The Sample %	State of Washington %	United States %
Education			
7 years or less	5	5	11
8 years	6	7	9
9-11 years	13	17	20
12 years	39	35	32
13-15 years	15	15	11
16 or more	22	21	17
	100	100	100
Total Family Income			
Under $3,000	4	2	3
$3,000 to $5,999	5	5	7
$6,000 to $9,999	34	22	25
$10,000 to $14,999	34	39	36
$15,000 to $24,999	18	26	23
$25,000 or more	5	6	6
	100	100	100
Occupation			
Professional, et al.	20	21	16
Managers (except farm)	22	14	14
Clerical	5	6	7
Salesman	6	7	7
Craftsman	16	23	23
Operatives	13	15	19
Service Workers	5	5	6
Farmers and Laborers	11	4	4
Laborers (nonfarm)	2	5	5
	100	100	101

NOTE: Data are from U.S. Bureau of the Census, Detailed Characteristics, 1970, Tables 148, 174, and 198 (Washington); Tables 199, 226, and 250 (United States).

1970 compared to the rest of the states and to the United States as a whole.

Occupationally, the sample includes more proprietors and managers and more farm owners and workers than state or United States and fewer craft workers. The greater proportion of farm people reflects differences between the county and the state. Eleven percent of the employed males in Yakima County work in agriculture—the same proportion is in the sample. The fact that the sample includes more proprietors and managers and fewer craft workers may mean no more than that many are self-employed and were classified in that category rather than in their craft, but we cannot be sure.

The sample possesses some advantages and some major limitations. It was drawn randomly from a geographical area with known limits. In this respect, it is more than an accidental or convenience sample. Perhaps a stronger point is that it obtains role data from both men and women and, since the men and women are from ths same marriages, the male and female respondents are in the same social classes, are living with the same number of children, and are roughly similar in some other social characteristics. Thus, male-female and husband-wife comparisons can be made with confidence within the overall limitations of this sample.

The limitations are at least equally great. Although the sample and the population from which it is drawn are similar in demographic characteristics, there is no way to determine how similar or different they are in role beliefs and behavior. The sample is from a single county with obvious limitations there. Finally, 210 cases is too small a sample to merit some types of complex analysis which will be needed before many questions concerning role norms and enactment will be answered. As indicated above, the data represent a testing ground for the conceptual and measurement strategies and provide a small body of initial findings. Later, larger samples will be necessary to answer a good many questions which this initial study poses.

PART II

**NORMS, BEHAVIOR AND
PSYCHOLOGICAL PROPERTIES**

Chapter 3

THE SOCIALIZATION AND CHILD CARE ROLES

Viktor Gecas

The two roles examined in this chapter, socialization and child care, have frequently been considered the mainstays of the family as a social system and as an institution. A frequent claim heard is that the family in America has lost many of its functions, such as economic, religious, educational, etc. But although other functions may vary, that which appears as the irreducible element of the structure known as the family is the nurturant socialization of children. Socialization and child care, then, are not only important functions which the family performs, they may be considered as the *definitive* elements of the family (see Reiss, 1965; Weigert and Thomas, 1971, for an elaboration of this view).

There is a certain logic in discussing the socialization role and the child care role in the same chapter, although their empirical and to some extent conceptual treatments will be handled separately within this chapter. Socialization, in our usage, is limited to the social and psychological development of the child. It refers to those processes and activities within the family which contribute to developing the child into a competent, social, and moral person. Specifically it involves such activities as teaching children what is right and wrong, developing in them a sense of responsibility, developing competence in eating and dressing properly, in doing school work, and generally in interacting with others. The particular manner or style of parent-child interaction, such as the amount and kind of discipline, support, and communication characteristic of the relationship, is also an aspect of the socialization process which may be consequential to the products of this process.

While socialization refers to the development of the child's social and psychological capacities, the child care role refers to the physical and psychological maintenance of the child. Activities such as keeping the child clean, fed, and warm, as well as protected from physical dangers and frightening experiences would fall within the child care role. Obviously, a good deal of socialization takes place while the child is being cared for and vice versa. Behaviorally, these two roles overlap. Yet they refer to conceptually distinct activities and may even be segregated according to the persons responsible for each.

Typically, however, the roles of socialization and child care have been closely linked to a particular status in the family—the status of parent. It is, therefore, instructive to look at the situation and circumstance of parenthood in the United States in a consideration of child care and socialization roles. Unfortunately, most of the research in this area has dealt with the consequences to the child of parent-child interaction. Much less frequently do we see the parents as the focus of attention. The few studies that have looked at the effects of children on parents have tended to find that these effects are quite pronounced (Rheingold, 1969; Osofsky, 1970; Devor, 1970; Bell, 1968). LeMasters (1974), for example, described the transition to the status of parent as a crisis for the individual and the marriage, since it involves a realignment of old roles, the adoption of new ones, and the redefinition of previous family relationships.

From the perspective of role theory (or role analysis), there are a number of factors which make the transition to parenthood (and the status of parent) more problematic in our society than is adjustment to marital and occupational roles. One of the best elaborations of this position is offered by Rossi (1968). She identifies four characteristics of parenthood which make it a difficult status for individuals.

(1) Cultural pressures on married persons to assume the role are great, especially for women. Rossi maintains that motherhood is the major transition point in a woman's life:

On the level of cultural values, men have no freedom of choice where work is concerned: they must work to secure their status as adult men. The equivalent for women has been maternity. There is considerable pressure upon the growing girl and young woman to consider maternity necessary for a woman's fulfillment as an idividual and to secure her status as an adult [1968: 30]

Rossi also points out that the psychological consequence of this cultural pressure on the woman to have children is that "latent desire and psychological readiness for parenthood may often be at odds with manifest desire and actual ability to perform adequately as parents" (1968: 29). This psychological tension may take the form of anxiety, guilt, and frustration over parenthood.

(2) Becoming a parent is not always a voluntary act. It may be the unintended consequence of a sexual act which was engaged in for totally different reasons. By contrast, one is much less likely to stumble into marriage. This difference in the modes of entering parenthood versus marriage implies that there is a much higher probability of unwanted pregnancies than of unwanted marriages in our society (Rossi, 1968: 31). Furthermore, as LeMasters (1974: 51) points out, parents do not choose their children (unless they adopt). They are stuck with the responsibility for their children whether they find them congenial or not. Some parents wind up with all boys when they would love to have a girl, with dull kids, tempermental kids, etc. They must accept what chance or fate provides.

(3) The parental status is relatively irrevocable. Once we enter this status, we are usually tied to it for life. We have become relatively free to leave an unsatisfactory job or even a marriage. But once a person has become a parent, there is little possibility of terminating that status, except in the rare instance of placing children for adoption. As Rossi put it, "We can have ex-spouses and ex-jobs but not ex-children" (1968: 32).

(4) There are few roles in society which are as poorly defined and for which people come as poorly prepared as those associated with parenthood. Training for parental roles is informal and sporadic at best. The advice of "experts" in child development is often contradictory, confusing, inconsistent, and frequently unsubstantiated by empirical research. And the expectations for the parental roles are very high. As LeMasters (1974) states, it is

not good enough for parents to produce children that are as good as they are; they have to be better than their parents. But the problem is that the guidelines for what constitutes a good parent and what kinds of parent-child interactions will produce the best offspring are rather vague and ambiguous. As a result, new parents not only enter their new status unprepared, but typically operate in an information vacuum (Brim, 1959, for empirical support of this assertion; in LeMasters, 1974: 50).

In addition to these role problems of parenthood discussed by Rossi, LeMasters (1974: 50) suggests that there is a romantic complex surrounding parenthood which is even more unrealistic than that relating to marriage. This common idealization depicts children as cute and parenthood as fun. Martha Wolfenstein (1963) has documented the emergence and development of this theme in Infant Care Bulletins over the past two decades. This preconception of prospective parents may make them even more ill-prepared for children and parenthood when they do occur.

But most people do manage to survive as parents, and some even flourish in these roles. How mothers and fathers negotiate the socialization and child care roles within the normative system which they perceive and help define, how they evaluate their performance of these roles and describe the conflicts and strains that they experience, as well as the satisfactions will be the focus of the present chapter.

THE SOCIALIZATION ROLE

NORMATIVE DEFINITIONS

Traditionally, the mother has been more closely associated with child-rearing and child care than has the father. The traditional division of labor in the family has the domestic roles (house-keeping, child care, and child socialization) as the major domain of the wife-mother, and the provider role as the primary activity and responsibility of the husband-father. Zelditch (1955), using the parallel concepts of expressive and instrumental roles, found this sexual division of labor to hold cross-culturally. And, as we noted earlier, Rossi considers motherhood to be the most central role for a woman in our society. Therefore, is spite of the increasingly egalitarian ideology of conjugal relations that has been characteristic of the United States, we would still expect the social norms to stress that child socialization is a greater responsibility of the mother than of the father.

To get at the norms regarding socialization, we identified a number of specific tasks involved in the socialization role and asked the respondents their opinions on who *should* have responsibility for doing each task. There were five response categories provided, ranging from Husband Always to Wife Always. Surprisingly, the findings presented in Table 3.1 indicate that *the norms* regarding most of these socialization tasks are largely egalitarian—that is, the most frequent response category is the one which gives father and mother the same responsibility for the task. This is most evident for the task of teaching children right from wrong. Ninety percent of the fathers and ninety-three percent of the mothers responded that this responsibility should be equally shared by fathers and mothers. Comparing the means for the various tasks in Table 3.1, we note that there is a slightly greater expectation for the father to discipline children and to teach them responsibility. Mothers, on the other hand, are favored in the most concrete of the tasks, teaching children to eat and dress properly— forty-nine percent of the fathers and seventy-two percent of mothers indicated that it was more the wife's responsibility than the husband's. Comparing the responses of husbands and wives across all of these task items we find that there is a consistent tendency for each spouse to credit more of the (normative) responsibility for a task to his (or her) sex than is credited them by the opposite sex.

ROLE SANCTIONS

The strength of the norms governing the performance of the socialization role is indicated by the sanctions people would impose on those who were perceived as not adequately performing this role. We asked husbands and wives to respond to the following question: "If a woman didn't teach her children the things they need to know in order to be able to take care of themselves and in order to get along with others, how would you act toward her and

Table 3.1
HUSBAND AND WIFE REPORTS OF SOCIALIZATION NORMS AND ROLE ENACTMENT (in percentages)

NORM: Who Should Teach the Following Tasks?	TOTAL		Husband Always		Husband More Than Wife		Husband and Wife the Same		Wife More Than Husband		Wife Always		MEAN*	
	H	W	H	W	H	W	H	W	H	W	H	W	H	W
To Eat and Dress Properly	100	100	0	0	2	0	47	23	50	73	1	4	3.51	3.80
To Get Along with Others	100	100	0	0	4	0	87	90	9	10	0	0	3.06	3.10
What is Right and Wrong	100	100	0	0	5	1	92	94	3	5	0	0	2.98	3.03
To Learn To Take Responsibility	100	100	0	0	15	7	80	88	5	5	0	0	2.89	2.97
To Help in School Work	100	100	0	0	5	8	67	63	27	28	1	1	3.25	3.21
Discipline Children	100	100	0	0	17	13	76	78	7	9	0	0	2.89	2.97

ENACTMENT: Who Teaches Children?	TOTAL		Husband Always		Husband More Than Wife		Husband and Wife the Same		Wife More Than Husband		Wife Always		MEAN*	
	H	W	H	W	H	W	H	W	H	W	H	W	H	W
To Eat and Dress Properly	100	100	0	0	2	0	26	20	68	71	4	9	3.73	3.90
To Get Along with Others	100	99	0	0	7	2	63	59	30	37	0	1	3.23	3.38
What is Right and Wrong	100	100	0	0	7	2	75	73	17	25	1	0	3.12	3.24
To Learn To Take Responsibility	100	100	0	0	20	14	58	60	21	25	1	1	3.02	3.13
To Help in School Work	100	100	0	0	10	20	24	25	58	49	8	6	3.60	3.37
Discipline Children	100	100	0	0	25	15	50	46	24	38	1	1	3.00	3.24

*Mean scores are based on the following weights: Husband Always = 1, Husband More = 2, Husband-Wife Same = 3, Wife More = 4, Wife Always = 5. Scores above 3.0 indicate the wife should or does enact the role more than the husband.

her family?" Less than twenty percent of husbands and wives said that they would be indifferent to this situation. The rest indicated that they would impose some kind of sanctions (ostracism) on the negligent parent. The most frequent sanction was not to choose the person as a close friend—seventy-two percent of the wives and sixty percent of the husbands mentioned this. Approximately fifteen percent of the respondents selected the strongest sanction category, "would not want the person in the same neighborhood." In general, wives responded somewhat more strongly on these sanctions than did husbands.

ROLE ENACTMENT

The difference between what should be done and what actually is done is the difference between norms and behavior. The data show that the most common division of labor regarding social-ization tasks is equalitarian, but not nearly as equalitarian as the norms would have it. The most equally shared tasks in the social-ization role appear to be those dealing with the moral and social development of the child: learning right from wrong, learning to take responsibility, and learning to get along with others. Between fifty and seventy-four percent of the respondents stated that they and their spouse were equally involved in these tasks. However, for each of the socialization tasks the frequency distributions are skewed toward the wife's side of the scale, consistently more so than was the case for socialization norms. All of the mean scores for the tasks are over 3.00 (which would be an equal division), except for disciplining children as reported by husbands. This indicates that the wife is more involved in child socialization than is the husband. More wives state this to be the case than do husbands. So, while parents say that the socialization role *should* be largely performed by both husband and wife, in practice the wife winds up performing a larger share.

The sex of the child has frequently been found to be an important variable in parent-child interaction (Lynn, 1969). Parents not only have different expectations for boys and girls, but they define relationships with their child differently de-pending on the sex of the child (Table 3.2). Fathers are reported (by both fathers and mothers) to take more responsibility for the

Table 3.2.

SOCIALIZATION OF BOYS AND GIRLS
(in percentages)

	TEACHES BOYS		TEACHES GIRLS	
	Husbands' Report	Wives' Report	Husbands' Report	Wives' Report
Husband Entirely	1	2	0	0
Husband more than Wife	25	21	4	1
Husband and Wife the Same	39	33	28	25
Wife more than Husband	33	45	65	71
Wife Entirely	2	0	4	3
TOTAL (%)	100	101	101	100
Mean	3.11	3.21	3.67	3.76

socialization of boys than of girls. Mothers are reported as having greater behavioral involvement in socializing girls than boys, although it should be noted that mothers have slightly more involvement than fathers in the socialization of both girls *and* boys. This tendency for greater parental role enactment in the teaching of their same-sex child is more frequently reported by the parent regarding his or her own behavior than in reporting that of his or her spouse.

Parents reported receiving some help in the socialization role from other family members, extended kin, and non-relatives. The category of persons most frequently utilized for this purpose is older children in the family. Forty-eight percent of wives reported that at least "a little" help in the socialization of the younger children was received from the older brothers and sisters. Grandparents were second in importance as sources of help with socialization (thirty-two percent of wives said they helped a little or more). Non-relatives were next (twenty-four percent) and other relatives provided some help according to ten percent of wives. Wives consistently reported greater participation of these categories of people in child socialization tasks then did husbands. Since the wife is more heavily involved in the socialization role, her perception of the participation of non-parents in this role is probably more accurate than the husband's. All in all, however, parents do not seem to receive much help from others in the performance of this role—only nine percent of wives reported that "much of these activities" were performed by others. This is congruent with the finding (discussed later) that parents would be reluctant to "hire a well-trained person" to help with child socialization. Parents seem to feel that the child socialization role not only belongs in the house, but that it should be performed largely by the parents themselves.

STYLE OF ROLE ENACTMENT

Most of the discussion of child socialization so far has focused on the content of the role—e.g., what is done, and who does it. But there is another important dimension of this role, the *style* of role enactment, or the strategies parents use in enacting the socialization role. To get at the issue of style of role enactment, we asked parents how they would respond to the child under three sets of circumstances stated as follows: (1) "What kinds of things do you do to get your child (age 8-10) to do something you want him to do?" (2) "If your child is playing and accidentally breaks something that you value, what would you do?" and (3) "If your child intentionally disobeys after you have told her to do something, what would you do?" These were intended to measure strategies to obtain compliance, punishment for accidental misbehavior, and types of punishment for deliberate misbehavior.

The four most frequent response categories for husbands and wives in getting the child to do something are to ask or request the child, to tell the child, to reason with the child and explain why he or she should do it, and to bribe by giving or promising a reward (these categories are not mutually exclusive). An interesting difference between the responses of husbands and wives is that the most frequent strategy for mothers is to ask their children to do something (forty-two percent), while fathers are most likely to tell them to do something (thirty-seven percent). Mothers are also more likely to reason with the child than are fathers. For that matter, mothers use more strategies in getting the child's compliance than do fathers. For all but three of the response categories they showed higher frequencies, while fathers were more limited in their responses and also more appeared somewhat authoritarian.

Table 3.3.

PARENTAL RESPONSE TO CHILD ACCORDING TO CIRCUMSTANCES OF THE CHILD'S BEHAVIOR BY HUSBAND'S OCCUPATION (in percentages)

	Situation 1: Child Accidentally Breaks Something				Situation 2: Child Intentionally Disobeys				Differences Between 1 and 2			
	White-Collar		Blue-Collar		White-Collar		Blue-Collar		White-collar		Blue-Collar	
	H	W	H	W	H	W	H	W	H	W	H	W
Scold and/or Yell	47	75	37	56	30	49	32	32	17	26	5	24
Reduce Allowance	3	3	2	5	2	2	4	4				
Ignore Behavior	2	2	1	1	1	0	0	0				
Discuss Problem	62	70	56	51	17	20	15	16	46	49	41	35
Make Child Guilty	6	6	10	5	6	6	10	2				
Keep Reminding Child	5	3	4	2	5	7	2	2				
Refuse Privileges	17	14	19	11	54	55	41	55	37	41	22	44
Spank or Slap	19	18	28	21	65	67	70	55	45	50	42	34
Withdraw Affection	3	1	0	0	5	0	0	0				
Isolate Child	2	3	0	0	6	14	5	3	4	11	5	3
Other	4	1	0	1	1	2	1	0				
(N) =	(107)	(107)	(93)	(93)	(107)	(107)	(93)	(93)				
Sum of Differences									149	177	115	140

We asked parents what they would do if "your child is playing and accidentally breaks something that you value?" Over fifty percent of mothers and fathers indicated that they would not punish the child, but would discuss the problem with the child. Slightly more fathers than mothers said they would use physical punishment—e.g., spank or slap the child. But the most frequent response of the mothers under this circumstance is to scold or yell at the child, which was a comparatively frequent category for the father as well. Scolding and yelling as well as discussing the situation with the child may be viewed as reprimanding the child for an act that may not be the child's fault. They represent relatively lenient reactions.

The last circumstance, however, is viewed by parents as a more serious transgression. The question as posed asked: "If your child intentionally disobeys after you have told her to do something what would you do?" The majority of both fathers and mothers said that they would physically punish the child. Another fifty percent of the parents would punish by refusing privileges to the child. A surprisingly low proportion of parents (two percent of fathers and none of mothers) said that they would use withdrawal of affection as a means of punishing the child. This is surprising considering the amount of attention this technique has received by scholars, and the extent to which it has been used to describe child discipline practices of American families (see, for example, Bronfenbrenner, 1970; Green, 1960).

SOCIAL CLASS VARIATION

Research dealing with social class variations in the style of socialization (child-rearing) has consistently shown that since World War II, middle-class parents have become progressively more permissive in child-rearing than have lower-class parents. Bronfenbrenner (1958) attributed this trend to the influence of professional advice through mass communication, such as Dr. Spock's (1957) book on child care, and the differential exposure of mothers in different social classes to this source of information. Middle-class mothers would be more likely to seek out and be influenced by professional advice on child-rearing than would lower-class mothers. This professional advice, Bronfenbrenner argued, reflecting strongly the neo-Freudian influence, stressed permissiveness coupled with love in child-rearing, as opposed to the preceding philosophy emphasizing constraint, discipline, and the dangers of "sparing the rod and spoiling the child." Wolfenstein (1963) documented this shift in values from a "duty-oriented" to a "fun-oriented" socialization, in her content analysis of advice to mothers given (from 1914-1951) in the Infant Care Bulletin of the Children's Bureau. And it is middle-class parents, better educated and typically more isolated from interaction with extended kin because of greater mobility, who were more likely to take this advice to heart.

But is there anything about social class per se which might affect the content and style of the socialization role? Kohn (1963, 1969) provides the most elaborate discussion of the link between the occupational structure (the most commonly used indicator of social class) and the socialization role. He states that members of different social classes, by virtue of experiencing different conditions of life, come to see the world differently, develop different conceptions of social reality, different aspirations, and different conceptions of the desirable (1963: 472).

In discussing the conditions of life distinctive of these classes, Kohn (1963) identifies three ways in which middle-class occupations (white-collar) differ from lower-class occupations (blue-collar). First, white-collar occupations typically require the individual to deal more with the manipulation of ideas, symbols, and interpersonal relations, whereas blue-collar occupations deal more with the manipulation of physical objects and require less interpersonal skill. Second, white-collar occupations involve much more self-direction in the performance of work, while in blue-collar occupations the individual is more subject to the standardization of work and to direct supervision. Third, economic advancement in one's job is more likely to call for individual action by white-collar workers, while in blue-collar occupations it is more dependent on collective action (e.g., union activity). As a result of these differences between the conditions of white-collar and blue-collar occupational structures, two basic value orientations emerge. White-collar workers are more likely to enunciate values dealing with self-direction, such as freedom, individualism, initiative, creativity, and self-actualization; while blue-collar parents are more likely to stress values of conformity to external standards such as orderliness, neatness, and obedience. Kohn, in fact, did find that the white-collar and blue-collar parents he studied did differ in this expected direction. Parental values, then, tend to be extensions of the modes of behavior that are functional for parents in their occupational structures, and they become apparent in the content of socialization.

Kohn also maintained that these value orientations are reflected in the style or circumstance of parental discipline. Because of the greater emphasis white-collar parents place on self-direction and internal standards of conduct, they are more likely to discipline the child on the basis of their interpretation of the child's *intent* or motive for acting as he or she does. Blue-collar parents, on the other hand, are more likely to react on the basis of the *consequences* of the child's behavior. They are apt to punish the child when his or her behavior is annoying, destructive, or disobedient.

We are able to address this theoretical issue by comparing parental responses to the child under two sets of circumstances: (1) when the child accidentally breaks something that the parent values, and (2) when the child intentionally disobeys the parent. According to Kohn's hypothesis, middle-class parents should be more discriminating in their responses to the child between situations one and two, while lower-class parents should be more uniform in their responses across the two situations.

Our findings, presented in Table 3.3, give modest support to this hypothesis. Combining the percentage differences between circumstances one and two for the five most common response categories, we find that the differences are greater for white-collar parents than for blue-collar parents. In other words, the responses of white-collar parents are slightly more discriminating with regard to the circumstances of the child's behavior than are those of blue-collar parents. The largest difference score was found in the responses of middle-class mothers (177 percentage points), while the lowest occurred for lower-class fathers (115 points). In general, wives were more discriminating than husbands. Looking at the specific response categories, we find that the largest percentage differences for both classes and sexes of parents occurred in he "discuss problem," "spank or slap," and to a lesser extent "refuse privileges" categories. In the situation where the child accidentally breaks something, parents are much more likely to discuss the event without punishing the child—this is especially true of middle-class mothers. But when the child intentionally disobeys the parent, he or she is more likely to receive physical punishment or restriction of privileges. Again, these discriminations are greater for middle-class parents than for lower-class parents.

The differences found between blue-collar and white-collar parents in response to the child's behavior are paralleled by differences between parents of different educational levels. This type of consistency is not too surprising since education is related to social class status and is even used as an indicator of social class. There is a tendency for college-educated wives and their spouses to discuss the problem with the child when the child's behavior is accidentally disruptive and in general to more frequently reason with the child as a strategy of behavior control. Wives with high school education or less and their spouses were more likely to resort to physical punishment and scolding the child under these circumstances.

Comparison of education levels gives even stronger support to Kohn's hypothesis than was the case for occupation—e.g., there is a greater difference between parental responses to the child in situations one and two for college-educated parents than for those of high school education. The highest difference score, for five of the most frequent response categories, is found for college women (summary difference = 197); the lowest is found for husbands of high school wives (D = 126). The difference is larger for women than for men, a difference of sixty-five points between the summary scores of wives in these two education categories versus a difference of thirty-four points for husbands.

ROLE COMPETENCE

On the question of competence in the performance of the socialization role, parents rated themselves rather favorably. The question was stated as: "All things considered, how effective do you think each of you are [sic] at teaching your child the things he or she needs to know in order to be able to take care of him- [or herself] and get along with others?" Over two-thirds of the husbands rated themselves as either "extremely effective" or "quite effective" in performing this role, and seventy-four percent of the wives fell into these categories. It is interesting to note that respondents were evaluated higher by their spouses than by themselves. These favorable evaluations of role competence are probably related to the strong parental identification with the role and the high value placed on its performance. It would be psychologically damaging to be considered by self or spouse to be incompetent in a role that is both important and largely unavoidable for parents.

ROLE STRAIN

In discussing some of the difficulties of performing the parental role in our society, LeMasters (1974: 18-30) reviews some of the folklore associated with parenthood: "that rearing children is fun," "that children improve a marriage," "that all married couples should have children." But perhaps the most anxiety-producting bit of contemporary folklore associated with parenthood is the one that states: "There are no bad children—only bad parents," and its corollary, "Children will turn out well if they have 'good' parents." These two beliefs about parenthood place a considerable burden on parents to "succeed" at child-rearing, because if their children turn out "bad," blame will fall on the parents. This condition, coupled with some of the other problematic aspects of parenthood mentioned above (especially the lack of consistent guidelines of what to do in the role), could be expected to produce a good deal of strain or anxiety in many parents about their performance of the socialization role.

Our findings support this expectation (Table 3.4). We asked respondents the following question: "All things considered, how well do you think you do at teaching your children how to take care of themselves and how to get along with others?" Fully twenty-five percent of the wives and sixteen percent of the husbands said that they worry frequently and wish they would do better. It seems that wives are more worried about their performance in this role—fifty-four percent of wives compared to forty-five percent of husbands worry about it to some extent while only four percent of wives (six percent of husbands) indicated complete satisfaction with their performance. This suggests that the socialization role may be more central to the wife's position than it is to the husband's, and the responsibility to do well is more a burden

Table 3.4.

ROLE STRAIN REPORTED BY MOTHERS AND FATHERS IN THE
CHILD SOCIALIZATION AND CHILD CARE ROLES (in percentages)

SOCIALIZATION: How well do you do teaching your child?

	H	W
Worry frequently, wish I would do better	16	25
Worry once in a while	29	29
Don't think much about it either way	4	1
Usually feel I've done a good job	38	37
Completely satisfied with the way I teach them	6	4
No response	7	4
TOTAL (%)	100	100
Mean*	2.88	2.63

CHILD CARE: How well do you do caring for the physical needs of your child?

	H	W
Worry frequently, wish I would do better	10	8
Worry once in a while	14	15
Don't think much about it either way	4	1
Usually feel I've done a good job	50	59
Completely satisfied with the way I care for them	18	14
No Response	4	3
TOTAL (%)	100	100
Mean*	3.53	3.57

*High score indicates absence of worry and positive satisfaction with one's performance of the role.

for the wife. This interpretation is given greater credibility by the finding that husbands of employed wives worry more than husbands of unemployed wives—perhaps because they have greater responsibility for child socialization when the wife is employed.

ROLE IDENTIFICATION

There was a good deal of consensus between husbands and wives that the socialization role should be performed by family members. In response to the question: "If you had a very large income for life making it possible for you to hire a well-trained competent person to help you [socialize] your children, do you think you would do so?" Seventy-six percent of the men and sixty-four percent of the women said they probably would not. What is interesting here is that more men were opposed to the idea of hiring an outsider for this purpose than were women. Perhaps it is because mothers would be the chief beneficiaries in obtaining help with the role.

To some extent this item may be used as an indicator of the degree to which the individual indentifies with the socialization role. Reluctance to relinquish the role even when economically possible and normatively permissible indicates a certain amount of psychological commitment to the role and perhaps satisfaction in performing it. If we can make this methodological inference, then we can say that our findings show that parents have a high level of identification with the socialization role. This is congruent with self-concept studies which have shown parental identities (father, mother) to be among the most important elements of an individual's self-conceptions (Gecas, 1973; Lopata, 1971).

ROLE CONFLICT

Compared to other roles, there is considerable disagreement between husbands and wives over matters dealing with the enactment of this role. Seven percent of the mothers reported frequent disagreement, thirty-seven percent "sometimes," forty-six percent "seldom disagree," and only ten percent said they never disagree. The husbands' responses were very similar. This is higher than for any other role (compare Table 9.8).

When there is disagreement, it is interesting to note, the husband is more likely to have the final decision. If we consider who makes the final decision in an area of disagreement as an indication of conjugal power, then it would appear that the husband has more power than the wife, even in a family role which behaviorally is more the wife's domain than the husband's.

THE CHILD CARE ROLE

NORMATIVE DEFINITIONS

The distinction between the activities involved in child socialization and in child care is not always obvious. Both involve intimate contact with the child, and activities engaged in for one purpose—i.e., feeding the child—can have implications for the child's socialization—i.e., learning appropriate norms for eating. There is also overlap of roles in the other direction—teaching children to be competent is caring for them in the most effective way, by enabling them to care for themselves.

In spite of this overlap between child socialization and child care, there are basic differences between the two roles which warrant separate consideration. We have already noted that socialization deals with the development of the child's social and mental capacities, while the focus of child care is providing the physical and psychic care of the child. The object of the former role is to produce a socialized person. The object of child care is to enable the development of a healthy organism. It is fairly obvious that the tasks involved in the socialization role are more complicated, more variable, more subject to frustrations, and have more unpredictable outcomes than are the activities making up the child care role, some of which are mechanical and routine.

There is another difference between the two roles. They are not isomorphic in importance or in emphasis over the time span of parent-child interaction. When the offspring is an infant, care of the physical needs is of critical importance, and this characterizes most of the activities of the parent with respect to the infant. As the child grows and develops greater physical and mental skills, the parent's socialization role takes on greater importance. Therefore, when we speak of child care and child socialization, the referent for the former is typically a young child.

CHILD CARE NORMS

Perhaps because of this, the mother in American families has been more closely associated with the child care role than has the father. The infant's early and total dependence on others, the practice of breast feeding, and the tendency for the wife to have greater responsibility for domestic activities while the husband works outside the home make it more practical for the wife to have greater responsibility for child care. We would expect this division of labor to be even more strongly weighted toward the maternal side than was the case for child socialization. Lopata's (1971) research indicates this to be the case even in families that share these activities. She states:

The fact that so many respondents feel that their husbands "help with the children" is significant, even when stated as a form of praise. It suggests that child care is not part of the role of father and is done as a favor to the wife [1971: 121].

We defined the child care role for our respondents as activities which keep the child clean, fed, and warm, protected from frightening experiences and from dangers which might cause physical harm. Then, to get at the normative division of labor, we asked, "Who should take care of the physical needs of your children?" Our findings show that child care is perceived as more the wife's responsibility than the husband's by both husbands and wives, but more so by wives:

	Husbands	Wives
Husband and wife should have equal responsibility	62%	44%
Wife should have more than husband	27%	51%

But when we broke the child care role down into its component tasks, we found considerable variation in the division of responsibility across these tasks (Table 3.5). Wives were perceived to have major responsibility for keeping children clean, fed, and warm; and husbands perceived themselves as having greater responsibility for the physical protection of their children. Wives, however, thought this task as well as protecting the child from frightening experiences should largely be shared equally between husband and wife. We also find in these normative responses, as with the socialization role, that husbands and wives assess *themselves* more responsibility for each task than is assessed them by their spouses.

SANCTIONS

Parents place a high value on the child care role, as indicated by the strength of the sanctions that would be imposed for nonperformance and by the perceived importance of the roles. In response to the question: "If a woman neglected the physical needs of her children how would you act toward her?" Seventy percent of the husbands and eighty percent of the wives said that they would not choose this person as a close friend. Only seventeen percent of husbands and fourteen percent of wives said this

Table 3.5
HUSBAND AND WIFE REPORTS OF CHILD CARE NORMS AND ROLE ENACTMENT (in percentages)

NORM: Who Should Perform the Following Child Care Tasks?	TOTAL		Husband Entirely		Husband More Than Wife		Husband and Wife the Same		Wife More Than Husband		Wife Entirely		Mean*	
	H	W	H	W	H	W	H	W	H	W	H	W	H	W
Keep Children Clean	100	100	0	0	1	0	22	6	70	83	7	11	3.83	4.05
Keep Children Fed	100	100	0	0	1	0	22	9	69	77	8	14	3.83	4.04
Keep Children Warm	100	100	0	0	2	0	41	25	52	66	5	9	3.60	3.84
Keep from Fright	100	99	2	1	13	4	69	75	15	20	1	0	2.99	3.14
Protect from Danger	100	100	3	1	24	8	63	77	9	14	1	0	2.81	3.03

ENACTMENT: Who Does each of These Child Care Tasks?	TOTAL		Husband Entirely		Husband More Than Wife		Husband and Wife the Same		Wife More Than Husband		Wife Entirely		Mean*	
	H	W	H	W	H	W	H	W	H	W	H	W	H	W
Keep Children Clean	100	100	0	0	2	0	10	9	73	71	15	20	4.01	4.12
Keep Children Fed	100	100	0	0	2	0	11	9	67	63	20	28	4.04	4.16
Keep Children Warm	100	100	0	0	3	1	24	24	60	55	13	20	3.81	3.94
Keep from Fright	100	100	1	0	8	4	58	48	30	44	3	4	3.26	3.46
Protect from Danger	100	100	2	1	21	10	57	56	19	30	1	3	2.98	3.23

*High scores indicate the role should be and/or is enacted more by the wife (see note to Table 3.1).

situation would "make no difference" in the way they acted toward the person. More wives expressed the use of sanctions for a mother's non-performance of child care, although most parents of both sexes would exact sanctions for nonperformance of this role. We also asked parents, "How important is it to you that the physical needs of your children are taken care of?" Not surprisingly, the overwhelming majority of parents of both sexes (over ninety-five percent) indicated that it was "extremely important." These findings indicate that a value is placed by parents on the child care role, as high as that placed on child socialization.

THE ENACTMENT OF CHILD CARE ROLE

On the normative questions, we found that the wife was expected to have greater responsibility in the child care role. With regard to the enactment of the child care role, the wife is even more heavily involved than the norms specify. A large majority of the wives and a smaller majority of the husbands reported that the wife does more than the husband in caring for the physical needs of the children (Table 3.5). Only nineteen percent of wives and twenty-nine percent of husbands said that this role was equally shared. Furthermore, on all of the specific tasks that were enumerated for the role, the wife is reported (by both husbands and wives) to have greater involvement than the norms specify. Again, the wife's heaviest involvement is with the tasks of keeping children clean (the modal response category was "wife more than husband"). The most equally shared task appears to be "protecting children from danger"—husbands report that it is equally shared, while wives indicate that it is the most equally shared of the five tasks, even though they still do more in this task than do husbands.

The reason for the differential perceptions of involvement in this task (as well as the task of "keeping children from frightening experiences") might be the tendency for fathers to see themselves as protectors of their family, morally and psychologically obliged to protect the family from physical dangers when they occur. However, serious physical dangers to family members which the fathers may perceive and would feel obliged to act on are relatively infrequent events compared to the daily dangers and mishaps which a child experiences and with which the mother, because she is there, must deal. This could be the reason she perceives herself as playing a more active part in this task.

ROLE COMPETENCE

Both husbands and wives perceived themselves and their spouses as quite effective in the child care role. The proportions of self and spouse ratings in the categories "quite effective" and "extremely effective" ranged from eighty-two percent to ninety-three percent, with wives getting slightly higher ratings from themselves and from their husbands. A sizable proportion, thirty percent, rated themselves and their spouses as "extremely effective." These competence ratings are higher than those found for child socialization.

ROLE STRAIN

There appears to be less strain involved for parents in the child care role than there was in the socialization role. Only twenty-four percent of husbands and twenty-three percent of wives reported that they worry to some extent over their performance in the child care role. By contrast, it will be recalled that fifty-four percent of the wives and forty-six percent of the husbands worried about their performance in the socialization role (Table 3.3). This difference between the two parental roles is understandable. The criteria for assessing adequacy of performance and the standards of evaluation are more clear-cut in the child care role than they are in the socialization role. Also, the outcomes of parental activity are much more predictable in child care (if the child is not fed, he or she will get sick) than they are in child socialization (what should a parent do to produce a happy, secure, productive child?). For these reasons, child care is a psychologically easier role to perform than is the socialization of children and so we would expect less strain and parental self-doubts in the former role than in the latter.

ROLE CONFLICT

There is less frequent conflict reported by parents about child care than there was for child socialization, and for some of the same reasons, we suspect, that we mentioned in discussing role strain. Seventy-five percent of husbands and eighty-four percent of wives indicated that they disagreed "seldom" or "never" about child care. This is in contrast to fifty-nine percent of husbands and fifty-four percent of wives responding in these categories for child socialization (see Table 9.8).

There is also a difference between child care and child socialization roles regarding the resolution of role conflict. When overt disagreements between parents do occur about matters of child care, the wife has as much influence in the final decision on the disagreement as the husband. The responses of husbands and wives were almost identical: the mean responses on "who makes the final decision if there is a disagreement about child care" were 2.94 reported by husbands and 2.99 reported by wives (a mean of 3.00 indicated that husband and wife have equal influence, while a score above 3.00 would favor the wife and below 3.00 the husband). We could suggest that the greater power of the wife in this role, compared to the socialization role, is related to her greater performance with child care as well as her greater responsibility for the role.

SOCIAL CLASS AND SITUATIONAL VARIATIONS IN THE SOCIALIZATION AND CHILD CARE ROLES

Family literature is rich in the description and analysis of social class differences in child socialization and care (Bronfenbrenner, 1958; Kerckhoff, 1972; Hess, 1970). Likewise, such behavior has been found to vary by family size, by family life cycle, and by the employment of the mother. The effect of these variables on our several dimensions of parental roles are examined below.

SOCIAL CLASS VARIATION

In general, the sociological literature would lead one to expect more equalitarian norms, role enactment, and power in the middle class (for example, see Kirkpatrick, 1963), with less conflict, but perhaps more role strain (see LeMasters, 1974). However, our data show equalitarian norms for sharing socialization and child care roles are about equally shared in the blue- and white-collar families, with similar variations across the specific tasks. Nevertheless, there were some social class differences. Blue-collar parents were less likely to be interested in sharing child socialization or child care roles with nonfamily members, but also less likely to provide sanctions against those who enact the role poorly. Seventy-two percent of middle-class mothers compared to sixty-three percent of lower-class mothers indicated that they would not choose as a close friend a "woman who did not teach her children the things they need to know in order to take care of themselves and to get along with others."

Commitment of mothers to the performance of the child care role was felt somewhat more strongly by lower-class than by middle-class women. White-collar mothers were more favorably disposed to hire "a well-trained person to take care of their children" (forty percent answered they might or they would) than were mothers in blue-collar families (twenty-seven percent). The responses of husbands were more negative than those of their wives and very similar between the two social class categories. These findings are parallel to those of Swinehart (1963) who found that middle-class mothers are less accepting of the "service aspects" of the maternal role than are lower-class mothers. The child care role subsumes a large part of these "service aspects" of motherhood.

With regard to role strain, the conceptual (Goode, 1959) and to some extent empirical family literature suggests that the upper classes are more concerned about their performance of the parental roles than are the lower classes.

Our own findings, however, do not support this social class difference. The blue-collar parents in our sample reported worrying about as much over their competence in the role (fifty-four percent of mothers and fifty-one percent of fathers worried at least occasionally) as did the white-collar parents (fifty-five percent of mothers and forty-six percent of fathers).

Overall, the social class similarities in role norms, enactment, and strain in the socialization and child care roles are more impressive than the differences, and even where differences were found they were not always consistent with previous literature.

EMPLOYMENT OF THE MOTHER

We find small but consistent differences in the direction of greater sharing of socialization tasks by husbands and wives when the wife is employed. This is consistent with other research showing that, in households where the wife is employed, there is a greater tendency to share household chores with the husband (see Blood and Wolfe, 1960; Hoffman and Nye, 1974). Exchange theory provides an explanation for this finding: When the wife takes on some of the provider role, and thereby helps out in a role which is primarily the husband's, distributive justice would place a burden on the husband to take a greater share in some of the roles more closely associated with the wife—e.g., housekeeping and child-rearing. And if the sense of justice does not bring about a greater sharing of domestic tasks, then the constraints of time and efficiency may, since a working mother would be less available for domestic duty.

FAMILY COMPOSITION

An appreciable literature has led to the anticipation of role differences by diversity in ages of children, by age of parent and by family size. With respect to child socialization and care, some of these differences, although usually not very large, are found in our data. Younger parents seem to identify more with the parental role, in that more reject the idea of having a "well-trained person" to assist with it. Fifty-two percent of the wives under thirty responded "certainly wouldn't" compared to twenty-six percent of those thirty to thirty-nine years of age. Another age difference, somewhat surprisingly, is a greater specialization in socialization tasks among young parents, with wives taking greater responsibility for teaching children to eat and dress properly and husbands disciplining and teaching responsibility. A similarly greater segregation is found among young parents in fathers teaching boys and mothers girls, than is true of older parents.

Worry over child-rearing increases with family size, especially for fathers—twelve percent of the fathers of families with "under four children" reported that they "worry frequently" compared to twenty-nine percent of fathers of families with "over five children." The difference was not as large for wives, but it was in the same direction. Mothers, however, are more affected by the presence of preschool children in the home—thirty-three percent reported "worrying frequently" compared to nineteen percent of mothers with school-age children. Fathers of preschoolers also worried slightly more than fathers of school-age children. These differences are even more pronounced for the child care role.

More disagreement was reported in families with preschool children present, especially by the husband. Fifty-nine percent of fathers with preschool children reported disagreeing at least "sometimes" with their wives over the socialization role, compared to thirty-two percent of fathers with school-age children. The presence of preschoolers may be a more trying time of the family life cycle for parents, since we also found that they tend to worry more about their adequacy in performing this role. It might also be that spouses work through their disagreements over a period of years.

The presence of preschool children in the home also had an effect on the perceived normative responsibilities of husbands and wives. In families with preschoolers present, the wife was expected to take greater responsibility in all of the child care tasks (by both husbands and wives) than in families with school-age children only. This is to be expected since preschoolers are in the mother's care during the day.

CONCLUSION

In this chapter, we have examined two roles associated with parenthood—child socialization and child care. The former focused on activities related to the social and psychological development of the child, the latter dealt with the child's physical maintenance. We explored these roles from a number of different angles and dimensions: the normative, behavioral, evaluative, and conflict aspects as perceived by husbands and wives. We also looked at variations across several independent variables—i.e., social class, education level, wife's employment status, wife's age, family size, and stage in family cycle.

It would be difficult to locate these findings on the child care roles historically, since we do not have comparable studies from the past. But we suspect that the image of these roles which we have presented is a temporal one. If the study had been done thirty years ago, we suspect that we would have found the husband's participation in these roles much less than we find presently. And there is enough instability in the current family picture to warrant speculation about future changes in family roles. The direction of change seems to be toward the greater sharing of tasks in the child care and socialization roles, and, concomitantly, the comparative decreasing involvement of the wife. There are a number of social forces currently operating on the American family. The women's movement is the most visible and most clearly identified with a value position calling for the redefinition of sex roles and the realignment of the relationships between the sexes toward a more egalitarian model. We find this existing at the normative, but not at the enactment level.

There are other changes taking place in the larger society which may be less conspicuous but most important in the long run. We only have space to mention some of these: (1) overpopulation and the increased emphasis on smaller families—made technologically possible by more efficient birth control methods, which will decrease the time and effort invested in these roles; (2) the reduction of housekeeping chores over the years because of smaller families and modern technology; and (3) an increasingly more favorable employment picture for women desiring work outside the home. Some social observers have gone so far as to say that motherhood and housekeeping roles are becoming obsolete as an occupation (Bernard, 1972; Binstock, 1972). We are not prepared here to support this level of speculation (in fact, our data on role identification question this), even while we are tempted to muse about the future of socialization and child care roles.

Chapter 4

THE KINSHIP ROLE

Howard M. Bahr

Two of the most widely accepted generalizations of the sociology of family life are that kinship obligations exist and that
their scope and nature vary both within and between societies.
The literature is full of examples of behavior from which the
existence of norms about family obligations may be inferred,
and sometimes there are explicit statements about the norms
which govern interaction with kindred. For example, Farber
(1964: 196) lists as characteristics of "ideal kindred relations"
norms relating to (1) participation in rituals and ceremonies, (2)
promotion of the welfare of family members, (3) making personal resources available to family members, (4) trust in the
kindred, and (5) maximizing communication.

Another dimension of the kinship is the salience or importance of kinship obligations as compared to other family roles.
Despite the body of recent literature attesting that kinship obligations and interactions are viable in modern urban society (see,
for example, Adams, 1968, 1970; Litwak and Szelenyi, 1969;
Sussman and Burchinal, 1962), there is wide support for the view
that the context and perhaps the extent of kinship interaction has
changed. It is argued that the family has "lost" certain functions,
and that kinship structures are now weaker or less important than
they once were. Farber (1964: 188) summarizes this point of

view, noting, "The reduction in the importance of extended kinship structures in contemporary societies implies that they continue to exist mainly for 'emotional' and sentimental reasons." If such a reduction has occurred, an assessment of the relative salience of kinship norms is most timely. There has been little effort to establish the strength of the norms governing kinship relations, or to measure the degree to which nonperformance is perceived as worthy of sanction. Since the viability of kinship responsibilities has been challenged, this chapter will treat the existence of "the kinship role" as hypothetical and will examine, for some aspects of the role, people's ideas about whether performance is obligatory or optional.

NORMATIVE DEFINITION OF KINSHIP ROLE

Several researchers have directly or by implication dealt with the normative structure of modern nuclear families. Reiss (1962: 336) found that ninety percent of his middle-class Bostonites agreed that "people have an obligation to keep in touch with kin." Women were more apt than men to express an unqualified positive kinship obligation. Older people were apt to report that they did not see enough of their relatives, in contrast to persons in the early stages of the family cycle who typically said that they saw enough of their relatives. Almost half of the sample pointed to family rituals (wedding, christenings, funerals, etc.) as a chief reason for family contact, and Reiss concluded that "the *obligation* to attend such an event or answer such a need is determined by degree of relationship; culture norms of extended kinship *obligations* do influence interaction to this extent" (1962: 337, italics added). However, he noted that only a small proportion of interaction with kin could be accounted for by such obligations to special family events.

Leichter and Mitchell (1967: 19) include the notion of kinship obligation as an essential part of the definition of kinship bond:

Kinship *bonds* are ties of obligation and sentiment between those in specific reciprocal statuses. The concept of bond implies that certain relationships within a network are accorded a *priority*, and that this patterns the organization of the network; that is, stronger bonds serve as links for other relationships . . . for certain purposes some kinship ties are given priority.

Most of their respondents (377 clients of the Jewish Family Service of New York) affirmed that there were strong obligations for interaction with kin. Sixty-three percent agreed that "it is selfish for someone to cut himself off from his relatives" and seventy-two percent agreed that "regardless of what brothers or sisters may have done, one should never stop talking to them." Also, despite a strong emphasis on success, almost all (ninety-one percent) agreed that "even if some relatives are much better off than others, that shouldn't stop them from getting together as often as they can" (Leichter and Mitchell, 1967: 73-75, 129, 217). Relevant to our own indicators of communication with kin are Leichter and Mitchell's (1967: 104-105) comments about obligations for interaction between kin:

> Kinship values clearly entail the obligation to maintain contact with kin by telephone as well as other means. . . . Failing to communicate by telephone is as much a breach of kinship obligations as any other failure to interact. . . . Interview statements indicate views about obligations are often so strongly felt that telephone contact is maintained even when inconvenient.

The normative component of kinship ties was also tapped in Adams (1968: 80, 82) study of married residents of Greensboro, North Carolina. He reported that a sense of "ought to" or obligation was cited as an important reason for maintaining kin contacts: Eighty-five percent of the respondents affirmed some kind of obligation as an important reason for keeping in touch, ranging from forty-eight percent to sixty-five percent, depending on expressed emotional closeness and the residential location of the parents.

As indicated above, the kinship *role* is treated as hypothetical. Evidence for its existence would be: (1) affirmation by a majority of married persons of the existence of obligations or duties to kindred, and (2) sanctions for nonperformance. In the present study, the assessment of obligation was based on the question, "Who, if anyone, has a duty to do the following for your own relatives?" There followed a list of four tasks: (1) make decisions of financial help or economic assistance, (2) write letters to relatives, (3) telephone relatives, and (4) visit relatives.

Our findings show that the large majority (approximately three-fourths) of husbands and wives affirm an obligation to kin and report feelings of disapproval for nonperformance of kinship obligations. There are no differences between wives and husbands in the recognition of these obligations to kindred, but more wives express strong disapproval for noncommunication with kin. The fact that at least three-fourths of both wives and husbands would sanction nonperformance of kinship role obligations is evidence that the role exists.

Also notable are the contrasts between rates of affirmation and proportions of respondents prescribing sanctions. On the "financial aid" items, the existence of the norm is more apparent in the willingness to sanction nonperformance (seventy-seven percent of the husbands said they would mildly or strongly disapprove, as did seventy-nine percent of the wives) than in the affirmation of an obligation (sixty-six percent of the husbands, fifty-nine percent of the wives). On the other dimensions of the kinship role (duty to visit or telephone kin), wives are as willing to apply sanctions as to affirm a duty to kindred, while husbands are significantly more apt to affirm the duty (ninety percent) than to prescribe negative sanctions for nonperformance (seventy-four or seventy-five percent). Thus, the dimensions of normative behavior vary, depending upon whether one looks at prescriptions or sanctions. The proportion affirming prescriptions may be either greater or smaller than the proportion prescribing sanctions, depending upon the type of behavior in question.

Let us now consider the other aspect of norm—*who* should enact the role. One of the well-substantiated findings about kinship in America is that wives tend to be more active than husbands in maintaining kin ties. In fact, Adams (1968) lists the greater involvement of females in kin affairs as one of only six established generalizations about urban kin relations in Western society.

Young and Willmott (1957: 57-58) noted the importance of having living parents, especially the mother, if ties among siblings are to be maintained. In their words, "The siblings see a good deal of each other because they all see a good deal of Mum." They also found that daughters' interaction with their mothers is more frequent than sons', and consequently sisters see more of each

other than brothers do of sisters or each other. Similarly, Leichter
and Mitchell (1967: 108-109) report that among Jewish families
wives communicate with kin more frequently than husbands,
perhaps partly because the task of communicating with kin is
delegated to them:

> Wives are to some extent delegated the task of 'representing' the family
> in kin contacts. They are responsible for relaying what goes on with kin
> to their husbands, so that husbands are also involved in kin interaction
> on the telephone through their wives.

The delegation to women of responsibilities for maintenance of
kinship ties has also been remarked by Robins and Tomanec
(1962: 345), who suggest:

> The greater closeness to female relatives can probably be explained by
> the fact that women tend to act as the representatives of the nuclear
> family in fulfilling obligations to relatives.

Moreover, an examination of kinship interaction and communication among migrant families in the Cape Kennedy region of
Florida (Berardo, 1967) revealed that females play the dominant
role in kin communication processes. For one thing, when husbands crossed state lines to visit relatives, they usually went to
visit the wife's parental home. Second, wives were more apt than
husbands to write or to telephone relatives, or to receive communication from them. Also, women's roles in establishing and maintaining kinship ties were demonstrated by deterioration of
extended kinship relations following death of the wife:

> If the mother ... had survived, then the frequency of interaction with
> kin was almost as high as when both parents were alive. The role of the
> father apparently has little import with regard to the maintenance of
> extended family relations; the interaction level of subjects with a
> surviving father was almost as low as when both parents were deceased
> [Berardo, 1967: 553].

Further evidence of the importance of the wife in maintenance
of kinship relations is evident in reports of types of kin interacted
with most frequently. Leichter and Mitchell (1967) report that, in
terms of absolute frequencies of interaction, wife's mother, sister,

and brother headed the list, followed by husband's sister, brother, and mother.

These reports from other researchers led us to expect that (1) both husbands and wives would define maintenance of kinship ties as more the responsibility of the wife than the husband, and (2) performance of the role would reflect more activity by wives than by husbands.

The response categories to our question, "Who, if anyone, has a duty to . . ." ranged from "husband entirely" through "husband and wife exactly the same" to "wife entirely." There was also a category called "optional—but it should be done," suggesting that the kinship obligations devolved upon the couple, but not specifically upon either spouse. Responses to the question are summarized in Table 4.1. The mean scores in the last row of the top portion of the table represent an index of the extent to which each activity is assigned to the wife, based on a 5-point scale with "husband entirely" counting 1 point, "husband and wife exactly the same" 3 points, and "wife entirely" counting 5 points. Thus, the hypothesis that families define the four activities listed as more the wife's than the husband's responsibility will be supported if the mean scores are higher than 3.0, the point at which the role is numerically defined as exactly shared between the spouses.

It is clear from Table 4.1 that the maintenance of kinship ties is defined as sex-specific role behavior. Only about ten percent of the husbands and wives who stated that kinship obligations existed claimed that the responsibility for these obligations could be assigned without reference to sex of spouse.

On matters relative to financial assistance of relatives, the husband is accorded principal responsibility even when it is the wife's relatives who are under consideration. Visiting relatives is defined as a responsibility to be shared fairly equally by both spouses, although the wife is somewhat more responsible for visiting her relatives than the husband is for visiting his. But with respect to maintaining communication via letters or telephone calls, the major responsibility for communicating *with the husband's relatives* is ascribed to wives, and, of course, they are also expected to maintain ties with their own relatives. In brief, financial decisions tend to be defined more as the husband's role, but communication with kindred is defined as largely the wife's responsibility.

Table 4.1.

NORMATIVE DEFINITIONS AND ROLE ENACTMENT OF THE SEXUAL DIVISION OF LABOR FOR KINSHIP ACTIVITIES, AS REPORTED BY HUSBANDS AND WIVES (in percentages)

NORM: Who, if anyone, has a duty to do the following for your own relatives?

	Make Decisions on Economic Assistance		Write Letters to Relatives		Telephone Relatives		Visit Relatives	
	Wife	Husband	Wife	Husband	Wife	Husband	Wife	Husband
Husband entirely or mainly	27	37	1	12	3	20	2	11
Husband and wife exactly the same	55	49	12	16	25	31	66	69
Wife entirely or mainly	7	4	82	59	60	36	23	9
No prescribed sexual division of labor	11	10	5	12	11	12	10	11
Total (%)	100	100	100	99	99	99	101	100
Total (N)	113	127	177	177	177	178	175	180
mean scores*	2.66	2.52	4.21	3.66	3.82	3.19	3.27	2.98

SANCTIONS: How would you feel about a couple who do not do the following things for or with their relatives (presuming their relatives would have liked them to)

	HUSBANDS REPORT		WIVES REPORT	
	Strongly Disapprove	Mildly Disapprove	Strongly Disapprove	Mildly Disapprove
Don't give financial help or economic assistance in crises	40	39	32	45
Don't write or telephone	45	42	33	42
Don't visit	45	41	33	41

*Scores are based on "husband entirely" = 1, to "wife entirely" = 5. Means are based only on those respondents prescribing a sexual division of labor.

ROLE ENACTMENT

The indicators of role enactment in the kinship role stem from three questions. The first question was: "Families differ in the things they do with or for their relatives. Please list below the main ways your own family is now involved with their relatives." What do our respondents do with relatives? Visiting and recreation account for about seventy percent of all interaction, with fifteen percent communicating by letter and telephone, accounting for most of the remainder (Table 4.2). Husbands reported less varied involvement than wives. Husbands list 236 separate activities, compared to 292 activities mentioned by wives. However, the distribution by type of activity was very similar to that for wives (see Table 4.2).

Seventeen percent of the husbands and fourteen percent of the wives said they were not involved with their relatives in *any* way. But some who claimed noninvolvement did respond to questions about which spouse communicated with kin, or identified the relative contacted most often.

The second question refers to the division of labor by sex in role enactment, specifically responses to the question, "Who writes or telephones relatives?" The data show that wives provide most of the communication with husbands' relatives as well as their own. In approximately one-third of the families, the husband writes or telephones his relatives more frequently than his wife, and about one-sixth of the respondents said that communication with husband's kin was shared equally between spouses. But in half of the cases, it is the wife who does most of the communicating with husband's kindred, and almost always (eighty-four percent of the time) she is pre-eminent in interacting with her own relatives.

The third question on role enactment asked that respondents identify relatives with whom they had most frequent communication, and that they tell how often such interaction occurred. Each person was asked about communication with his or her own relatives, and then about communication with spouse's relatives.

The proportion of respondents noting some contact with relatives in response to this question ranged from a high of ninety-three percent (wives with their own relatives) to a low of eighty percent (husbands with wives' relatives). Our data show that the

Table 4.2.

PERCENTAGE OF HUSBANDS AND WIVES REPORTING VARIOUS TYPES OF INVOLVEMENT WITH RELATIVES

TYPE OF INVOLVEMENT	WIVES' REPORTS		HUSBANDS' REPORTS	
	Percent of wives reporting	Percent of all activities mentioned	Percent of husbands reporting	Percent of all activities mentioned
Visiting	66	43	56	42
Playing, recreation	41	27	31	23
Writing	11	7	11	8
Telephoning	9	6	10	8
Helping in emergencies	6	4	4	3
Aiding the handicapped, the aged	6	4	4	3
Business dealings	4	2	8	6
Babysitting	3	2	1	0
Living together	1	1	2	2
Other	6	4	7	6
TOTAL (%)	153*	100	134*	101
TOTAL (N)**	192	192	177	177

*Columns total more than 100% because some people reported more then one type of involvement.
**Represents the modal (N). Actual values ranged from 191-194 for wives and 176-177 for husbands.

tie between the wife and her family was the most common form
of kinship communication, followed by communication between
the wife and the husband's family, between the husband and his
family, and finally, between the husband and the wife's family.
However, we shall see later that more husbands interact *frequently*
with their wives' than with their own relatives.

For husbands, communication with parents, brothers, or sisters
accounted for ninety-four percent of their interaction with their
own relatives and ninety-two percent with their wives' relatives.
For wives, comparable figures were eighty-five percent for their
own families and eighty-four percent for husbands' families. Thus,
husbands' most frequent interactions with relatives tended to be
almost exclusively within their own or their wives' families of
orientation, but wives maintained a bit more frequent communication with relatives outside the immediate family.

Reports on frequency of interaction add further evidence of the
wives' greater involvement in communicating with kindred. Fifty-
two percent of the wives (compared to thirty-nine percent of
husbands) communicated with their own relatives at least weekly,
and ninety percent of them communicated at least monthly.
Husbands were more likely to have frequent contact *with their
wives' relatives than with their own* (forty percent reported
weekly communication with their wives' relatives, versus thirty-
three percent for their own relatives). The latter differences are
not statistically significant, but suggestive that the interests of the
wife tend to shape the interaction with kin.

STRESSES IN ROLE ENACTMENT

COMPETENCE IN ROLE ENACTMENT AND ROLE STRAIN

One set of stresses in role enactment stems from the disjuncture
between perceptions of normative prescriptions for the role—what
one feels he or she *ought* to do—and one's perception of what one
does. A question was asked about competence in role performance
and another on the respondent's personal reaction to his or her
performance. The competence question was phrased, "How well
do you feel that each of you meets your obligations toward your

relatives?" Responses ranged from "Better than any I know" to "The worst of any I know."

Husbands' and wives' responses to the first question were very similar, never varying more than three percent. The results show that most people think that their performance in this role is about average: Only one-fourth of the respondents rated their role enactment as above average, and one-tenth marked "not as well as most people." None of the wives and only one of the over two-hundred husbands described his performance as "the worst of any I know."

Responses to the question of personal assessment of performance indicated that some husbands and wives worry because their performance does not meet their own standards. Thus, while only nine percent of the wives said that their role performance was substandard, thirty-four percent said they worried "once in a while" or "frequently" because they thought they ought to do better at fulfilling their kinship obligations. More than twice as many wives as husbands stated that they worried frequently about their role performance. Husbands were more apt to state that they didn't think about it much one way or the other.

To summarize, most people in the sample said they did as well as other people in maintaining their kinship ties, and reported that if they thought about the quality of the kinship interaction at all, they felt their performance was average. Despite the fact that almost everyone said that they met their obligations as well as most people, one-fourth of husbands and one-third of wives said they worried about their performance in the kinship role. Apparently there is a feeling among some husbands and wives that their involvement with their relatives, while typical, is still unsatisfactory. This segment of the sample seems to be saying: I am as involved as anybody else, but kinship involvement in the wider society is not what it ought to be, and I worry that my own ties are too weak.

ROLE CONFLICT AND ITS RESOLUTION

There were two questions about marital conflict and the kinship role. One asked how often the couples disagreed on matters concerning the respondent's relatives, and the other asked how such conflicts were resolved. Husbands and wives reported comparable rates of conflict over kindred. About one-fourth of both husbands and wives reported conflict "sometimes" or more frequently, half reported conflict "seldom," and only one-fourth said they never disagreed about their relatives.

This represents a moderately high incidence of conflict (see Table 9.8), lower than child socialization and about equal to recreational, child care, and housekeeper. The conclusion that the kinship role ranks high as a source of marital conflict seems justified. Only the child socialization role consistently ranks higher as a source of conflict.

Resolution of overt disagreements over kindred indicates male dominance of the kinship role. When the disagreement is over his relatives, it tends to be the husband's decision; when it is over the wife's relatives, it is a shared decision. Considering only those respondents who reported some conflict, wives dominate (make the final decision "always" or "more often than husband") in only seven percent of the conflicts over husband's kindred and in twenty-two percent of the conflicts over their own kindred.

SUBCULTURAL AND SITUATIONAL VARIATION

Previous research suggests that there should be differences in norms and interaction in the kinship role in various social strata. For example, more emphasis on kinship obligations may be more typical of people reared in small than in large communities. Likewise, "situational variables" such as, for example, the employment status of the wife might be expected to affect frequency of interaction with kin. To assess the impact of these variables, we divided the husbands and wives into categories on several subcultural or situational variables, and compared rates of affirmation of kinship responsibilities and willingness to sanction nonperformance.

LOCALITY OF CHILDHOOD RESIDENCE

Are the rural-raised more kin-oriented than those socialized in the city? Not with respect to expressed obligations to write, telephone, or visit. In each residential (farm, rural non-farm, town, or city) category, eighty-five percent or more of both wives and husbands affirmed the existence of obligations to maintain communication with kindred. However, with respect to financial assistance, rural background made a difference: Husbands raised in rural areas were more apt to recognize an obligation to kindred than are husbands who grew up in urban areas. This differential did not appear for wives, however.

Persons raised on farms were also more apt to disapprove of noncommunication with kindred than persons raised in cities. For example, about two-thirds of the husbands raised in cities would disapprove couples who did not write, telephone, or visit their relatives, compared to eighty-five percent or more of husbands raised on farms. Thus, the expectation that kinship role norms and sanctions would be more generally internalized among those with rural backgrounds receives considerable support. However, urban men were more likely to report kinship role strain, that is, to state that their interaction with kin is less than it should be.

SOCIOECONOMIC STATUS

Among wives there was a direct relationship between family income and feelings of obligation to be of financial assistance to own kindred. The same relationship appeared among husbands, although not so consistently. For each of the other types of obligation, the high-income wives were more apt than other wives to recognize kinship obligations. Among husbands, this pattern did not appear.

For three of the four types of obligations, wives in the income category $7,500-9,999 were least likely to affirm kinship duties, and for the husbands the lowest rate of affirmation of kinship obligations appeared consistently in this income category. In short, the more financially affluent families, especially wives, were more apt to recognize financial obligations to kindred. The norms for kinship obligations, both for communication and assistance, were less apparent in the lower-middle income group ($7,500-9,999) than among other income groups.

There is an inverse relationship between socioeconomic status, as measured by income, education, or occupation, and the proportion of husbands who defined communicating with kindred as primarily a wife's responsibility. Thus, husbands with some college were much less likely to define writing or telephoning their relatives as the wife's responsibility than were other husbands, and were somewhat more likely to define these tasks as primarily the husband's responsibility. A similar pattern holds for family income: the higher the income, the less apt the husband was to define communication with his kindred as primarily the wife's duty, although even in families in the highest income category, thirty percent of the husbands said telephoning the husband's relatives was primarily a wife's responsibility, and forty-seven percent of the husbands defined writing to a husband's relatives as primarily her responsibility.

A tendency was found, especially among husbands, for better-educated respondents to sanction nonperformance more than less-educated. Husband-wife differentials were greatest among the least-educated, with wives manifesting higher rates of disapproval than husbands, especially for non-communication with kindred. Thus, more affluent and better-educated people are more likely to affirm kinship obligations, and men in these categories are more likely to assume personal responsibility rather than considering the responsibility to be entirely or mainly the wife's.

Are there differentials by social class in perceptions of role competence and role strain? The analysis suggests a qualified positive answer. There is evidence of a positive relationship between family income and perceived role competence among both husbands and wives. An association between income and role strain is also apparent, but it appears to be sex-specific. For husbands, the higher the family income, the greater the role strain. For wives, the trend is in the opposite direction; the higher the family income, the *lower* the apparent role strain. Men in low-status blue-collar occupations were consistently lower than other men both in the affirmation of duties of the role and in the sanctions they provide to enforce prescriptions.

A greater proportion of educated women feel competent in the kinship role and fewer report strain. In contrast, among men the highest rates of role strain were reported by the best-educated men. While women with less education feel kinship responsibilities as strongly as do those with more education, a higher proportion feel inadequate in role performance. Similar patterns were found in the analysis of effects of occupational status.

EMPLOYMENT OF THE WIFE

Among wives who work, those who work forty hours or more are least apt to affirm kinship obligations, while those who work part-time are most likely to do so. Eighty-two percent of women who work forty hours or more weekly are less likely to affirm obligations to kin and less likely to feel remiss in their interaction with them. However, it is the part-time employed rather than the full-time housewives who are most kin-oriented in terms of felt obligation and concern about their performance. This curvilinear relationship was unexpected but may fit into other findings that the part-time employed are more integrated into group relationships with children and spouses (Hoffman and Nye, 1974), as well as (apparently) with kin.

Wives who work more than forty hours a week, and husbands who work more than forty-eight hours a week, tend to worry less about kinship relations than people who work fewer hours. The low incidence of role strain among the respondents who work very long hours suggests that one way to resolve strains in the kinship role is to expand the provider role. One who works unusually long hours either has less time to worry, or else worries about matters that seem more pressing than communication with kindred.

RELIGIOUS AFFILIATION

There were some small but consistent differences by religious preference. For every type of kinship obligation, those professing no religious preference were the least likely to affirm the existence of obligations to kindred. Similarly, persons reporting no religious affiliation were least likely to affirm sanctions for nonenactment of the kinship role. However, there were too few cases in the "no preference" category to justify generalization. These findings are suggestive only.

A higher proportion of fundamentalist Protestants express disapproval for nonperformance than do other Protestants or Catholics; the differences were smallest for the item involving economic assistance obligation. In fact, the rate of expressed disapproval for failure to communicate with or visit kindred was higher among fundamentalist Protestants than for any other social category, with the single exception of husbands raised on farms, for whom it was the same.

One of the more interesting findings about religious preference is that while the self-rated role competence scores of fundamentalist Protestant husbands are higher than those of either the Catholic or non-fundamentalist Protestant husbands, scores for their wives are lower than the scores of either Catholic or non-fundamentalist Protestant women. This simultaneous occupancy of the "highest competency" position by fundamentalist husbands and the "lowest competency" by their wives is intriguing, but the reason for it is obscure.

FAMILY SIZE

For each type of kinship obligation, parents with the smallest families (one or two children) were least likely to affirm kinship obligations, and those in the largest families (seven or more children) were the most kin-oriented. In general, there seems to be a direct association between number of children and affirmation of kinship obligations. However, the larger her family, the *less* likely a mother is to express disapproval over nonperformance of kinship duties. We have already argued that with a large family may come an increased need for support from kindred, and perhaps an increased sense of responsibility to have the children know their relatives. However, it may be that parents of large families acquire greater tolerance for diversity and norm infraction than do parents of small families. Another possibility is that a large family may make it difficult to manage the expected communication with kindred; a woman's willingness to overlook another person's nonperformance of obligations to communicate and visit kindred may reflect her own increasing difficulty in meeting these obligations. She may affirm the norm or even, as her family grows, affirm it more strongly, while at the same time becoming more tolerant of those who find it inconvenient to communicate or impossible to visit as they should. If this interpretation is accurate, people with large families should carry out their obligations to kindred less satisfactorily to themselves than do people with small families.

Perceived competence in kinship tasks varied inversely with family size. Thus, the proportion of women with seven or more children who asserted high competence was extremely low (nineteen percent). More apparent than the impact of family size on role competence, however, was its effect on role strain; only ten percent of the women with one or two children reported appreciable role strain in the kinship role, but about half of those with five or more children reported that level of role strain. The relationship between role strain and family size is clearly positive; the larger the number of children, the more the mother worries about her performance of kinship responsibilities.

IMPLICATIONS

The existence of a kinship role as part of the positions of husband and wife has been demonstrated on the basis of both perceived obligations to kindred and willingness to sanction non-performance of kinship responsibilities.

Rather than recounting the specific results, let us highlight the more important findings and their implications for future studies of kinship. First, it must be understood that the kinship role involves more than writing, telephoning, or visiting relatives although typically that is how it has been operationalized in research. Relatively few studies have paid attention to the sharing of economic or other family resources as a dimension of the kinship role, and still fewer have looked at the content and quality of communication with kindred, such as symbolic exchange via participation in family rituals, or the role of relatives as personal models or socializing agents.

The multidimensional nature of the kinship role is emphasized here because one of the findings in this chapter is that definitions of appropriate behavior by kindred, sex differentials in kinship responsibility, willingness to apply sanctions for nonperformance, and the impact of social background factors for the "economic assistance in crisis" task differs from those for other kinship tasks. To the degree that previous research has focused on frequency of communication and ignored aspects such as willingness to assume responsibility for rendering economic aid, it has considered only portions of the kinship role.

Present findings corroborate those of others that wives provide most of the communication with kindred. But our results suggest that wives do not dominate when the issue is making decisions about allocation of family resources, or conflict over kindred. In fact, the apparent female domination of the kinship role may stem largely from the husband's default or delegation of kinship tasks. He seems content for the wife to function as chief correspondent, executive secretary, or family clerk. But when the decision is whether to provide economic aid to relatives, or when there is overt disagreement, he is quite likely to make the decision. This was apparent in the responses of both wives and husbands. In fact, the apparent dominance of role enactment by wives may be largely a function of their having more available time than their husbands. The lesser enactment by employed mothers and those with large families suggest this. However, her enactment of the role develops relationships with her kin and neglects those of the husband.

The wife's enactment of the kinship role cements her family of procreation (including the husband) more firmly to her own parents and siblings than to the husband's family. The consequences of her general stewardship of family communication may be far more important for future family solidarity than the occasional instances when the husband asserts authority and makes an allocative or administrative decision.

The impact of background and contextual factors was found to vary by specific kinship task as well as by sex of respondent. Accordingly, as a rule, one should not refer to correlates of "kinship behavior" without referring to sex of respondent, or without being more specific about which components of kinship behavior are being considered. This finding suggests that much of the existing research on kinship is only partly accurate—that is, it applies to some components of the kinship role but not others, or holds for wives but not for husbands. For example, to talk about the effect of education on affirmation of kinship responsibility is likely to lead to errors unless one distinguishes the effect of education of wives' kinship orientation from that of husbands.

Another conclusive finding is that kinship behavior is defined as sex-specific. The nature of the division of labor by sex varies from family to family, but there is near consensus that it is a normatively defined division *by sex*. Only about one respondent in ten asserted that kinship tasks were matters about which the division of labor was optional rather than prescribed.

Several conclusions stem from the assessment of the effects of sub-cultural or situational variables. First, the relationship between number of children and kinship definitions and behavior merits further exploration. Women with large families were more willing to affirm kinship obligations, yet were less likely than other women to sanction nonperformance of these obligations. They were less likely to ascribe an equalitarian division to kinship responsibilities, less likely to rate themselves competent in the performance of kinship tasks, and more likely to worry about their performance. The crucial question is whether the generally less favorable kinship performance of mothers with large families primarily reflects family size per se, the lower-income or educational status of parents of large families, or other factors. Careful control of several socioeconomic factors is essential if this question is to be answered.

Finally, husbands reared in cities were less likely than other husbands to view interaction and help provided to kin as a set of duties required of them, and they were less likely to say they would sanction those who did not enact the kinship role. Their own ratings of their enactment of kinship tasks were less favorable than that of men living elsewhere, yet they reported more role strain than other men. The men with urban backgrounds were more apt to verbally reject the kinship role as a set of obligations, yet they cannot seem to rid themselves of some less explicit feelings of obligation. What may be needed is not abandonment of residential location as a predictor of kinship attitudes, but clearer specification of its underlying dimensions. It is possible that the important factors are neighborhood cohesiveness, proximity to kindred during childhood, or kinship relations in the family of orientation rather than community size or population density.

We have raised several questions. But the evidence for the existence of the kinship role, with attending norms and sanctions for nonperformance, is compelling. In practice, however, some ninety percent of interaction with kin is heavily concentrated in three areas: visiting, recreation, and communication by letter and phone. The prevalence in kinship behavior of sex-linked role prescriptions and sexually differentiated responses to comparable status situations has been demonstrated.

Chapter 5

PROVIDER AND HOUSEKEEPER ROLES

Walter L. Slocum and
F. Ivan Nye

The provider and housekeeper are among the well-established traditional family roles. In the provider role, goods and services needed by the family are produced or are obtained by an exchange of goods and services. The housekeeper role takes the goods and prepares them and maintains them for family use, including such cleaning or repair activity as may be required for their efficient use or conducive to the pleasure and comfort of family members. Thus, the two roles, besides having in common that they are traditional to the family, are complementary in an unusual sense that they usually involve the same goods at different points in their preparation and utilization by family members.

THE PROVIDER ROLE

Current laws and informal norms require a husband/father to assume the major responsibility for the support of the family if he is able to do so. It is clear, however, that actual performance of the provider role is no longer exclusively reserved for men; four out of ten married American women worked for pay in. 1970 according to the U.S. Census Bureau. Roughly, the same proportion of the wives in our sample reported earnings during the year preceding the interview.

NORMATIVE ASPECTS OF THE PROVIDER ROLE

Traditionally, in American society, the responsibility for providing necessary income has been assigned to the husband rather than to the wife. The legal system, by and large, supports this allocation of responsibilities; thus, the husband who is divorced or separated from the wife generally has to pay child support and/or alimony. Apparently most social scientists who have done research on family relationships also have taken the traditional role assignments for granted. However, some attention has been given to the effects of the employment of married women on intrafamily relationships. Nye and Hoffman (1963) presented the research available up to 1962 pertaining to the effects on the children, on the husband-wife relationship, and on adjustment of the employed mother. An updated summary volume of this work has recently appeared (Hoffman and Nye, 1974).

Aldous (1969) reported that, in working-class families, there tends to be a rigid division of labor which in effect reserves the provider role for the husband/father and the housekeeper and child care roles to the wife/mother. Sanctions, including withdrawal of rewards, are used by working-class wives to enforce these role prescriptions. In contrast, Aldous notes Rainwater's (1965) findings that in upper-middle-class families some roles may be shared. Hartley (1969) reported that her sample of forty working mothers had a tendency to view their employment as supplementary rather than primary. Thus, it appears from the literature that the basic cultural expectations remain. The husband/father is viewed as responsible for the provider role and the wife/mother as responsible for the housekeeper role.

With respect to normative prescriptions, respondents were asked to indicate how they would act toward a man and his family if he did not do his best to support his family. The pattern of responses was almost identical for both sexes. The overwhelming majority (about three out of four) of the respondents would not choose them as close friends, and less than one out of five checked the response category "It would not make any difference to me." Nevertheless, a pattern of tolerance showed up in other response categories: Thus, almost three out of four would not object to being in the same social group, almost three out of four would not object talking with them often, more than eight out of ten would not object to having them in the same neighborhood, and nine out of ten would not object to having their children play with the children of such a man. These responses may be interpreted to mean that outsiders' informal social sanctions for poor perfor- mance of the provider role by a married man are less severe than might have been anticipated.

This does not mean that abdication of the provider role by a married man would meet with approval. In fact, more than nine out of ten indicated strong disapproval of a hypothetical able- bodied husband or father who prefers to see his family supported by public assistance rather than work to support them.

We also probed for evidence of a normative prescribed provider role for the wife/mother, but found relatively little support for such prescriptions. One such probe was the following item:

"Mr. Jones makes an income the same as yours. Mrs. Jones is in good physical health, is twenty-five years old and has no children. Mrs. Jones doesn't feel it is her duty to work but Mr. Jones feels that since there are no children she should work outside their home. How do you feel about this situation?"

Only one man and two women felt that such a wife had a duty to work and only fourteen percent of the husbands and sixteen percent of the wives checked the response "It would be better if she found work."

Another probe was the following question:

"Should a wife work if her husband makes an income about equal to your income and they have children in school but no preschool children?"

Only one man and one woman checked the response category "It is her duty to go to work" and only six percent of the husbands and ten percent of the wives checked the category "It would be better in most circumstances for her to work."

A related question which dealt with a mother who is not a wife was worded as follows:

"If a woman with no husband has preschool children and good day care services are provided without cost if she takes a job, should she:

	Men (%)	Women (%)
stay home and accept Aid to Dependent Children support	7.1	9.0
take the job placing her children in the day care center	51.9	54.3
do whatever she personally would prefer"	38.6	32.9

The responses to this question suggest that there is a norm which requires a woman without the support of a husband to work, since more than half of both sexes indicated that she should take the job and place her children in the day care center. Most of the remainder would leave the choice up to the woman. There is not much support for the traditional idea that a woman should not be in gainful employment. Only seven percent of the men and nine percent of the women recommended that she stay home and accept ADC. Since whether the hypothetical woman was divorced, widowed, or the unwed mother of illegitimate children was not specified, it is not certain that the pattern of responses is entirely free of puritanical sentiments which might be directed toward the last of those. In any case, there was very little support for ADC among the respondents.

These questions all dealt with the provider role in families other than the family of the respondent. To obtain information about the normative aspects of the provider role in their own families, both men and women were asked the question, "With reference to your own family, who do you feel should provide the income?" The pattern of the responses is generally consistent with the prevalent views expressed in the literature. The husband is expected to be the main provider in the overwhelming majority of families. In fact, there was only one family in which both spouses said that the wife should provide more of the income than the husband and none in which either spouse felt that the wife should provide all of the income. However, there was a feeling in many families that the provider role should be shared; wives were much less likely (thirty-seven percent) than husbands (fifty-six percent) to insist that husbands should have the entire responsibility.

ROLE ENACTMENT: SHARING OF THE PROVIDER ROLE BY WIVES

As already noted, approximately four out of ten wives in the sample reported earned income. There are, of course, families in which the husband/father is unable to work for one reason or another. Our sample contained only three men who reported no earnings during the preceding twelve-month period (1969). However, an additional seven percent reported that their earnings during the previous year were less than $5,000.

The size of the sample places limitations on the number of categories for the analysis of sharing of the provider role. A dichotomy was drawn between families in which only the husband reported earnings during the preceding twelve months and families in which the wife also reported earnings. The distribution of families according to earnings was: wife has income—forty-four percent; reports no income—fifty-six percent.

CHARACTERISTICS OF FAMILIES IN WHICH WIVES SHARE THE PROVIDER ROLE

STATUS LEVEL OF HUSBAND'S OCCUPATION

Wives were most likely to be sharing enactment of the provider role if their husbands were employed in low-status blue-collar occupations and least likely to be sharing it if their husbands were in high-status white-collar occupations such as professions or management. More than half of the wives of high-status blue-collar workers (craftsmen and foremen) and wives of low-status white-collar workers shared the provider role. In view of the reasons for working noted later, this pattern appears to reflect the aspirations of families of lower-status (and hence lower-income) workers to attain levels of consumption nearer to those enjoyed by the families of higher-status, higher-paid workers.

EDUCATION OF WIVES

There was some tendency for wives with more education to be more likely to share the provider role. However, the relationship was not necessarily linear. The positive relationship between education and paid employment is generally consistent with national studies.

AGES OF CHILDREN

The contemporary American pattern of participation of married women in the labor force shows a relatively low rate of employment for women with preschool children; the rate rises as the children grow older. As a condition for inclusion in our sample, all of the families had at least one third-grade child, so we have a restricted range of possibilities insofar as this item is concerned. Our sample appears to conform to the national pattern insofar as it goes; mothers with preschool children were less likely (thirty-three percent) than those who had no preschool children (fifty percent) to share the provider role.

IMPACT OF WIFE'S SHARING OF PROVIDER ROLE

Although the earnings of wives in the families studied were usually much smaller than those of their husbands, they boosted total family income enough to permit the family to enjoy a considerably higher level of living. Median incomes in families with working wives were $11,750 compared to $10,315 in those in which the husband was the sole provider. Without the income of the wives, the median income of the families with working wives would have been only $8,717, more than $3,000 less than without the wife's contribution. Without the wife's contribution, these families would have had $1,600 less than the average; with it, they had $1,400 more (gross).

This is the stated primary objective sought by most working wives. A large majority of the working wives (eighty-three percent) indicated that their main reason for working was either to earn money to pay basic bills or to help reach family goals; twelve percent said their main reason for working was a feeling of accomplishment; four percent said they did so to keep busy; and two percent said they work to meet people. These responses correspond quite closely with those of earlier investigators. Sobol reported in 1963 that data from a nationwide sample showed that seventy-seven percent of wives worked because of family financial needs or to increase family assets (Sobol in Nye and Hoffman, 1963).

We conclude therefore that, whatever these women may have said about who should bear the major responsibility for family support, as a pragmatic matter they have consciously accepted a share of the provider role. The majority state that they have done so to enable their family to enjoy a higher level of living.

INCOME MANAGEMENT

It has often been said, although usually in jest, that men earn the family income so that their wives can spend it. Our data show that the most prevalent pattern is that the "income goes into a joint fund and is spent by both husband and wife;" this is the case in slightly more than half of the families; in twenty-two percent, the income is turned over to the wife; in an additional nine percent, the income goes to the wife who then gives the husband an allowance. Thus, in almost one-third of the families, the wife disburses the income. The entire income is managed by the husband in only seven percent of the families; in an additional nine percent, the husband gives the wife an allowance for household purposes and manages the remainder himself, for a total of about one family in six. Thus, the majority pattern is joint management but in families in which one spouse does it, is it more often the wife.

Contrary to expectation, working wives were not any more likely to manage the family income than other wives. There is no support in this study for the view that wage-earning wives or husbands who are sole providers are more likely to directly manage the family funds. There is even less support of the image of the man as the manager of the family funds. Present data suggest that the modern family, especially the younger family with third-grade children, is likely to be highly democratic where money management is concerned.

ROLE COMPETENCE

Female respondents were asked to evaluate their husband's performance of the provider role (Table 5.1). The responses reveal a clear tendency for wives to rank their husbands as better providers than the husbands rank themselves. There is also a noticeable, though less pronounced, tendency for men whose wives do not work to regard themselves as better providers than those whose wives are wage earners. Since they average higher incomes, this evaluation is well-founded. The same tendency is found among the wives; working wives tend to have a somewhat lower opinion of their husbands as providers than do nonworking wives. This is consistent with the reason for wives working that was noted earlier; most of them did so mainly because they felt that the family needed more income than the husband earned and the husbands of working wives average smaller incomes.

Table 5.1.

PROVIDER ROLE: EVALUATION OF HUSBAND'S PERFORMANCE
BY EMPLOYMENT STATUS OF THE WIFE (in percentages)

EVALUATION OF HUSBAND'S COMPETENCE	HUSBAND'S ANSWERS		WIFE'S ANSWERS	
	Husband only Earns	Both Earn	Husband only Earns	Both Earn
Exceptional	13.6	5.9	43.1	35.6
Better than Average	47.3	40.5	42.2	26.4
Average	37.3	48.8	12.8	33.3
Less than Average	0.9	4.8	0.0	4.6
No Job	0.9	0.0	1.8	0.0
TOTAL	100.0	100.0	99.9	99.9
TOTAL (N)	110	84	109	87

ROLE STRESS

The husbands were asked whether they ever worried about their performance as a provider. The responses indicate a higher incidence of worry among those whose wives shared the provider role (fifty-two percent) than among those who were the sole providers (thirty-nine percent). These responses are consistent with the responses to the preceding question. Considered together, these responses suggest that approximately half the husbands in our sample feel that they are not performing the provider role as well as they feel they should. We may say, therefore, that the role places a strain on men which they understand and acknowledge.

DISCUSSION

It seems clear that, in families interviewed, normative orientations toward the provider role are mainly traditional. Yet, at the same time, a large minority feel that the wife should also assume part of the responsibility for the provider role. The behavior patterns in families where the wife earns money for meeting family goals or to meet basic expenses go a long way toward allocation at the behavioral level of part of the responsibility for the provider role to the wife. These wives and others like them would find it difficult to give up their jobs because to do so would require their families to reduce their standard of living. Even though this is true, however, there were only a few families in which either husband or wife was ready to take the unequivocal stand that it is the duty of the wife to accept responsibility for all or part of the provider role if they have a capable, employed husband. The one exception to this surfaced in the reactions to the mother with preschool children but no husband where the majority of both sexes felt it was her duty to place her children in the day care center and go to work.

We may therefore conclude, both on the basis of what respondents say should be done and what they say they do, that women have secondary responsibility to perform the provider role in their families. We may also anticipate, on the basis of these circumstances and other developments such as the equal rights movement, that the old normative structure which placed the entire burden of family support on the husband/father is weakening and vulnerable to change.

THE HOUSEKEEPER ROLE

Housekeeping involves a set of responsibilities as old as the family itself, which stem from the capability of humans to prepare and cook food, mend and care for clothing and household equipment, and respond to concepts of cleanliness and order. Thus, the general activities included in the role are at least as old as the family, even though some of the specific forms that they take, such as obtaining the food at a supermarket, are distinctly modern.

Conceptually, the housekeeper role includes all of the instrumental tasks in food processing, cooking and serving, cleaning, laundering, repair of clothing and household equipment, marketing, and keeping the financial records relevant to these tasks. However, in societies in which the family is economically self-sufficient, marketing and financial transactions would not be involved.

It is important to distinguish between the housekeeper and housewife roles, the latter of which seems to include everything that wives usually do within the confines of the home. Depending on the family life cycle, the housewife role might include our child care, child socialization, housekeeper, sexual, therapeutic, recreational and kinship roles; that is, everything except provider (for a discussion of the housewife role, see Lopata, 1966).

NORMATIVE STRUCTURE

In most societies, most of the responsibilities of the housekeeper roles are allocated to the wife and/or mother, and this has been assumed to be true of the American family. Yet, how does this correspond with an increased ideology of equality between the sexes and the notion of maximizing the sharing of work and play? Present data suggest that the role is not quite as exclusively feminine as folk knowledge would suggest. A large majority of husbands (seventy percent) say that the role should be shared—not equally, with the wife carrying more of the responsibilities than the husband—but shared, nonetheless. Wives are a little more conservative in that only a small majority (fifty-five percent) agree that it ought to be a shared role. A few (less than two percent) believe it should be exactly equally shared, which leaves fewer than thirty percent of the husbands, and a little over forty percent of the wives who feel housekeeper responsibilities should be restricted to the wife and mother positions. Thus, *only a minority* of either sex view housekeeping as solely the responsibility of the wife.

The employment of the wife seems to modify the perception of both husband and wife concerning the sharing of the responsibility for the housekeeper role. If the wife is not employed, almost a third of the husbands and half the wives indicate that the housekeeper role is entirely the responsibility of the wife, but among couples in which the wife is employed, less than a fifth of the husbands and less than a third of the wives view the roles as entirely in the female domain (Table 5.2). Thus, there is more support for sharing the housekeeper than for sharing the provider role.

If some of the more specific responsibilities are listed separately, such as cleaning the house, care of clothing, preparing meals, shopping for groceries, and taking care of bills and accounts, the norms differ somewhat by tasks. A sizable majority (more than eighty percent of women and more than sixty percent of men) view care of clothing as entirely the responsibility of the wife. A small majority of women also report that cleaning the house and preparing meals should be done entirely by the wife, but less than half the husbands agree that the responsibility is entirely hers. Half of the husbands and wives consider shopping for groceries to be a joint responsibility, while only a minority of either women or men view taking care of bills and accounts as entirely or primarily the responsibility of the wife. Even so, more view it as primarily the wife's than as the husband's responsibility and, as we have seen, more women enact this part of the housekeeper role. Thus, most spouses feel that the care of clothing is entirely the wife's responsibility (and a majority of women would include cleaning the house as their sole responsibility). Preparation of meals and shopping are viewed as primarily but not entirely the wife's responsibility, while there is a wide range of opinion concerning who should take care of bills and accounts. It is possible that the lack of consensus on the latter point may be due to some respondents thinking of it as referring especially to household expenses while others included all family expenditures in responding to the question.

Table 5.2.

NORMS AND ENACTMENT OF THE HOUSEKEEPER ROLE BY EMPLOYMENT STATUS OF THE WIFE
(in percentages)

NORM: Who do you feel should do the housekeeping?

| | HUSBANDS' REPORT | | WIVES' REPORT | |
	Husband Only Earns	Both Earn	Husband Only Earns	Both Earn
Husband Only or Husband More	0.9	0.0	0.0	1.1
Both Same	0.9	2.4	0.0	3.4
Wife More	67.2	78.8	47.9	64.8
Wife Only	31.0	18.9	52.1	30.7
TOTAL	100.0	100.1	100.0	100.0
TOTAL (N)	116	85	117	88

ENACTMENT: Who does the housekeeping?

	Husband Only Earns	Both Earn	Husband Only Earns	Both Earn
Husband Only or Husband More	0.9	1.2	0.0	1.1
Both Same	0.0	3.4	0.0	2.2
Wife More	51.3	65.2	41.0	56.7
Wife Only	47.8	30.3	59.0	40.0
TOTAL	100.0	100.1	100.0	100.0
TOTAL (N)	115	89	117	90

SANCTIONS TO ENFORCE NORMS

As an indicator of the presence and strength of sanctions supporting the norms, respondents were asked: "If an able-bodied woman generally failed to keep her house clean how would you act toward her and her family?"

Women were more tolerant than men, perhaps feeling sympathetic for the slovenly housewife; sixty-two percent of wives compared to forty-three percent of the husbands said it would not make any difference. In contrast, some people evidently feel that housewives who do not keep their houses clean are disreputable. A substantial minority of the wives (thirty-one percent) and even more of the husbands (forty-seven percent) said that they would not choose slovenly housewives as friends and a few (six percent of wives and eleven percent of husbands) would not even want them in the same neighborhood. It appears, therefore, that substantial support in the form of sanctions remains for the housekeeper role, but that a large proportion of both sexes have less strong negative feelings about women who enact it badly.

Another question is relevant to presence or absense of sanctions to reinforce the housekeeper role—namely, the value attached to housekeeper role. Respondents were asked, "How important is it that housekeeping tasks are performed well?" About one-fifth responded "very important" and half "quite important" but more than one in four indicated it was only of some or even little importance. It would be illogical to expect people who view the role as relatively unimportant to become greatly concerned about those who do not enact it well. A small inconsistency in the value placed on a role and one's spouse's perceptions of one's value appears in the data. A larger proportion of men (twenty-nine percent) thought the role very important to their wives, but only nineteen percent of the wives indicated that it was very important to them. On the other hand, women underestimated its importance to their husbands. Only fifteen percent thought it very important to the husband, but twenty-one percent of the men reported it very important to them. These differences, however, are not statistically significant, and only suggestive that some lack of accuracy in spousal perception exists with respect to this role.

ROLE IDENTIFICATION

Relative to sanctions and to the value placed on the role is the degree of identification the position occupant has for the role. Respondents were asked: "Suppose you had a very large income for life, making it possible for you to hire a well-trained, competent person to help you with the above tasks. Do you think you would do so?" About half the wives indicate they certainly or probably would do so, and another quarter said they might. Only about one-fourth of the wives seem jealous of their enactment of the role. Thus, few women see the role as something they need to do personally, although a large proportion say it is important it be done well. Men are less interested in an additional person performing the role—only a fourth said they certainly or probably would add an assistant housekeeper. We shall see later (Table 5.2) that their participation in the role is quite limited so that they would have less to gain from such additional role-sharing.

ROLE ENACTMENT

Nearly all husbands and wives reported the role performed more by the wife than the husband (Table 5.2), but there is some disagreement over whether she does it all or the husband also participates. Whether the wife is gainfully employed influences the proportion of husbands who share the role. Thus, half the husbands of women who were not employed and two-thirds of those with employed wives report that they share the role, but some ten percent of their wives disagree and report that they (the wives) perform it entirely. Both sexes agree that more husbands of employed wives share the role—about fifteen percent more.

The enactment of several household tasks, care of clothing, cleaning the house, preparing meals, shopping for groceries and taking care of bills and accounts deviates at most points from the responses to the normative question of who should do them. The exception is care of clothing, where over eighty percent of the wives accepted it as entirely a feminine responsibility and about the same proportion state they do it without assistance. Some ten percent of husbands disagree, reporting they share these tasks. Otherwise, a considerably larger proportion of both sexes report that the wife performs the task (cleaning, food preparation, shopping, and bills) than earlier stated she should have full responsibility for the tasks. The differences vary between ten and fifteen percent who believe the role should be in part shared, but report the wife enacts it solely. The differences are especially great in disbursing money. About one-sixth of the wives and one-eighth of the husbands view this as entirely the wife's responsibility but about one-third of both sexes report the wife handles these tasks without participation from her husband and over sixty percent of both sexes report she discharges this responsibility more than does her husband. Thus, whether one views the role (Table 5.2) or component tasks within it, the ideology of role-sharing is considerably ahead of sharing in its enactment.

ROLE COMPETENCE AND STRAIN

Neither sex seems especially proud of its housekeeping performance. This might not be surprising for men, since the enactment of the role tends to be optional, but it is true also for a large proportion of women. Only six percent of the wives (five percent of the husbands) ranked themselves as "extremely good." The largest proportion of each sex (fifty-two percent of wives, and thirty-five percent of husbands) rated themselves "average." Eight percent of wives and over twenty percent of husbands evaluated their performance as poor or very poor.

From the previous discussions which disclosed that a considerable minority of each sex (1) place a low value on this role, (2) would not respond to nonperformance with sanctions, and (3) do not evaluate their own role performance highly, it might be anticipated that role strain, in terms of worry about one's performance, might be minimal. However, this is hardly the case. Nineteen percent of the wives frequently worry about their housekeeping, and twenty-nine percent do occasionally, or a total of almost half the wives. This means that, for women, strain in this role is equaled only by the therapeutic and exceeded only by the child socialization role (see Table 9.7). The explanation offered for the relatively high role strain is that self-rated competence is low (fifty-two percent rate themselves only "average"), role identification is very low, with only a quarter of the wives unwilling to share it with a paid employee, yet the value on a good performance is moderately high—about seventy percent rate it very or quite important.

CONFLICT

Husbands and wives both report relatively infrequent conflict in the housekeeper role. One in five wives and one in four husbands report verbal conflict "sometimes" or more often (see Table 9.8), while two in five wives and one in three husbands state there is never any open conflict over this role. As in other roles, more husbands than wives report conflict. If there is disagreement with respect to housekeeping, it usually is resolved in the wife's favor. Less than ten percent of either sex report decisions more frequently favor the husband.

SUBCULTURAL AND SITUATIONAL VARIATION

The general distribution of the role and its enactment is that it is either the wife's responsibility entirely or hers primarily, sharing it with her husband. The enactment of the role has followed the same general distribution, although the wife enacts more of it than the norms would allocate to her. As we have seen, the employment of the wife seems to increase the husband's share of the role both normatively and behaviorally.

SOCIAL CLASS

Men with more education (those with high school diplomas or more), are more likely to accept some responsibility for the housekeeper role, while those with less education are more likely to feel the role is entirely the responsibility of the wife. The relationship is not linear, however. Women with college degrees are also more likely to support a norm of shared responsibility, but other women with relatively high education are not more likely to do so than women with less than high school graduation. Women with college degrees and husbands with high school education or more are also more likely to report that the husband does enact the role. Therefore, these initial data suggest that both the norm and enactment of the role are shared by larger proportions of highly educated women (college graduates) and well-educated men (high school graduates or above).

RELIGIOUS PREFERENCE AND PARTICIPATION

Religious preference is unrelated to either the norm of role-sharing or enactment of the housekeeper role, but religious participation is related to both. Both men and women who never attend church are more likely to adhere to the norm of role segregation—that is, complete responsibility lodged in the wife. Among men, the relationship is linear, with the proportion adhering to the norm of a shared role increasing with frequency of attendance, but for wives, it is only those who never participate that appear to be more likely to adhere to the norm of a segregated housekeeper role.

FAMILY COMPOSITION

These data show that in families with three or more children both husband and wife are more likely to support a shared housekeeper role but the relationship is not linear. Those with five or more children are a little less likely to subscribe to role-sharing. This suggests that there may be a specialization in very large families in that women see household roles as their life and devote themselves entirely to it, rather than taking employment or seriously pursuing community activities. The data do not establish this, but are suggestive and agree with an earlier study on family size (Nye et al., 1970).

A curious difference between norms and behavior is found for families which include a handicapped person. In these families, husbands are less likely to subscribe to shared roles but, in practice, more do assist with the housekeeper role. It is not surprising that husbands would be "drafted," if necessary, to help with housework, but it is not obvious why they might feel they should not help. Perhaps these are families with "role overload," in that the husband has heavier responsibility for provider and child care roles because of the wife's responsibility for a handicapped person and therefore resists a duty to share housekeeping. Wives in these families do not differ in their normative beliefs, but those living with a handicapped person are more likely to report role-sharing by their husbands.

DISCUSSION

The provider and housekeeper are traditional familial roles which have long been taken for granted. Almost to the same extent it has been taken for granted that providing is the responsibility of husbands and housekeeping, of wives. Yet, the winds of change are all about. A majority of wives believe that they should share the provider role, and a majority of both sexes believe the husband should share the housekeeper role, but the data provide little evidence either of believing the roles should be equally shared or, in practice, that they are so shared. The proportion believing in or practicing equal role-sharing would be less than five percent. Some change may have occurred since these data were gathered, and these aspects of family roles (as well as all others) must be constantly restudied to determine whether and/or how much change may have occurred.

The prescriptions, values, and role identification differ considerably for the two roles. Sanctions against men who do not try to provide for their families are both generally held and severe in nature. Few people would fully accept such a man. Many also have a low opinion of a woman who neglects her housekeeping, but a substantial minority have little feeling about the enactment of this role. It would seem that the availability or nonavailability of substitutes probably explains the difference. A family can live in a messy house, can eat out of cans, or can use precooked foods, but if no one earns a living, they might starve or at least live at a marginal level. Perhaps a part of the difference, too, is in consequences for bystanders. A family living in a messy house, eating unappetizing food has few (more likely no) consequences for other families, but a family supported by Aid to Families with Dependent Children or other public funds is a financial burden on all other families.

Stated another way, there are a number of substitutes, in and beyond the family, for the housekeeper, but there is no accepted substitute for working husbands, even though some wives are employed. Substantially more men and women share the housekeeper role if the provider role is shared; this is reasonable, it seems, yet not all take that position (Table 5.2).

Relatively few women show any strong identification with the housekeeper role. A competent assistant would be welcomed by many. More men would hesitate to give up the provider role entirely.

Role strain is felt by large proportions of occupants of both roles. This is more surprising for the housekeeper role, since there is little identification with the role and many women evaluate their own role performance as mediocre. Yet, some seventy percent of both sexes indicate that an orderly and tidy house is quite or very important to them.

All in all, it appears that the housekeeper role is undergoing and may undergo still more basic changes. Most women identify little with it; husbands and children can easily share it, and the technology exists to have it performed by specialists—restaurants, laundries, and professional housecleaners. Therefore, as a primary responsibility of women, its days may, quite likely, be numbered.

6 1 4 4 7

THE SEXUAL ROLE

John Carlson

The sexual aspects of marriage have received a great deal of attention by researchers in a variety of disciplines, as well as popular writers and novelists. From the initial impacts of the Kinsey reports (1948, 1953) up to the more recent works of Masters and Johnson (1966, 1970), a great deal of effort has been made to understand the sexual behavior of males and females. On the popular side, numerous marriage manuals are available to provide people with information on proper sexual functioning. In addition to the Kinsey studies and the work of Masters and Johnson, researchers have studied the factors affecting frequency of marital coitus (Wallin and Clark, 1958a, 1958b; Clark and Wallin, 1964; Bell, 1971; Dentler and Pineo, 1960), and they have also looked at the relationship between sexual satisfaction and marital satisfaction (Wallin, 1960; Mowrer, 1954; Ellis, 1954; Gebhard, 1966; Pineo, 1961). In addition, a number of other variables have been studied in relation to sexual behavior.

However, most of these studies have lacked a conceptual framework and very few data have been utilized as a basis for developing a theoretical orientation to marital sexuality. The present study attempts to view sexual behavior within a role framework. That is, an attempt is made to determine the degree to which the spouses define their sexual behavior in terms of role prescriptions and proscriptions, and whether sanctions are provided for nonenact-ment. Some of the literature has implied the notion of role obligations in the sexual area of the family, although none have done so explicitly and completely.

ROLE IMPLICATIONS IN THE SEXUAL LITERATURE

Several writers discuss the relative duties of husbands and wives concerning sex but stop short of conceptualizing it as a role. Komarovsky (1962) found that a substantial proportion of the low-education wives in her study indicated that it is the wife's duty "to give it [sex] to her husband whether she likes it or not" (1962: 83). This finding reflects the traditional place of sex in marriage; one that places prescriptions and sanctions on wives, but not on husbands. However, Komarovsky found that a relatively large number of lower-class men expressed concern with their wives' sexual responsiveness and held themselves accountable for it (1962: 84). The notion of role obligations is implied here, but no further conceptualization is made. Similar findings emerge from Rainwater's (1965) study, in that many men expressed concern about their wives' enjoyment of sex. Again no attempt is made to place these findings into a role framework. Articles by Foote (1957) and Lewis and Brissett (1967) discuss sexual activity in terms of play and work. Foote argues that, with humans, sex is relatively divorced from procreation, especially with the advent of effective contraceptives, and becomes a form of play. Lewis and Brissett, on the other hand, argue that sex becomes tied to the work ethic with the strong emphasis on techniques and guidelines for sexual satisfaction. These authors base their argument on the numerous sexual manuals on the market. These manuals suggest that the husband does have a responsibility in satisfying the sexual needs of his wife.

As far back as the 1950s the husband's role in sexual activities was viewed as changing. Hacker (1957: 23) stated, "Virility used to be conceived as a unilateral expression of male sexuality but is regarded today in terms of the ability to evoke a full sexual response on the part of the female."

While several of these studies imply the possibilities of changing sexual roles, little research has specifically focused on sexual responsibilities utilizing a conceptual framework. They do report that many husbands have been concerned about sexual enjoyment by their wives, suggesting that values, norms, and behavior patterns consistent with the role concept are present in male sexual beliefs and behavior. However, these ideas and the research they have evoked have not, to the best of our knowledge, been conceptualized in terms of a sexual role. It is to this task of conceptualization and related operations of measurement and data reporting that the present report addresses itself.

NORMATIVE DEFINITION OF ROLE

It has traditionally been thought that husbands should initiate sexual activities and that wives who were overtly aggressive sexually were viewed as deviant. Our data suggest different feelings by husbands and wives as to who should initiate sexual activity. The largest proportion of husbands (forty-five percent) felt that both husbands and wives should have equal responsibility for initiating sexual activities, but virtually as many (forty-four percent) felt that husbands should have primary responsibility in that respect. Wives, on the other hand, responded quite differently, with about half feeling that husbands should have primary responsibility followed by a substantial number (twenty-six percent) indicating equal responsibilities, and a large proportion (thirty percent) who saw no duty involved.

In a role which requires mutual participation, such as the sexual role, this differential feeling as to who should initiate sexual activities could very easily lead to anxiety in sexual role performance, especially if sexual communication is lacking. It should also be noted that wives are much more likely to indicate that no one should initiate the sexual role. This may mean that wives do not care for sexual activity as much as their husbands. This finding is reflected in the responses to the question about sanctions against spouses who enact the role infrequently or not at all (Table 6.1).

Husbands indicate stronger disapproval toward both husbands and wives who do not consent to have sex than do wives. Almost twice as many wives (sixteen percent) as husbands (nine percent) have no feeling one way or another. At the same time, husbands

Table 6.1.

SANCTIONS AGAINST SPOUSE WHO RARELY CONSENTS
TO HAVE SEXUAL INTERCOURSE (in percentages)

ATTITUDE	HUSBAND'S REPORT		WIFE'S REPORT	
	Husband Who Refuses	Wife Who Refuses	Husband Who Refuses	Wife Who Refuses
Strongly Disapprove	81.3	78.9	65.5	67.3
Mildly Disapprove	9.1	12.2	16.8	16.8
No Feeling One Way or the Other	9.6	8.7	16.8	15.4
Approve	–	0.5	1.1	0.5
TOTAL	100.0	100.3	100.2	100.0
TOTAL (N)	198	208	191	202

indicate slightly stronger disapproval toward themselves than toward their wives. In other words, they are more likely to accept role refusal by a wife than by a husband. This again may reflect the feeling that wives have less interest in sex than have husbands. This question provides an additional indicator of the strength of the responsibility of spouses to engage in sexual activities. It is obvious that both spouses disapprove of those who refuse to have sex, but a larger proportion of men feel strongly about it.

Another aspect of the normative definition of the sexual role relates to its exclusivity within the marital relationship. This was measured by asking respondents how they felt about spouses engaging in extramarital activities.

Over eighty percent of husbands and eighty-five percent of wives strongly disapprove of extramarital sex under any circumstances. A higher proportion of husbands would support sanctions against wives than against themselves, but the difference is not statistically significant. This provides less support for the double standard than might be expected from popular myths. Over ninety-two percent of husbands and ninety-six percent of wives disapprove under most or all conditions.

In summary, these respondents hold conventional norms regarding sexual behavior in families. They feel that either the husbands should initiate sex or that it should equally be initiated by both spouses. Most respondents strongly disapprove of spouses who do not consent to sexual activity and almost all believe that sexual activity should be contained within the nuclear family. A substantial minority of women (sixteen percent) would not provide sanctions for spouses who did not participate in sexual activity with the spouse, yet only four percent of wives were permissive toward extramarital sexual activity. An appreciable minority, perhaps twelve percent, of wives see no need for sex either inside or outside marriage.

ENACTMENT OF THE SEXUAL ROLE

The initiation of sexual activity is viewed by both spouses as being a husband-oriented activity. Eighty percent of both spouses indicated that the husband initiates sexual behavior more than the wife. These findings are somewhat consistent with the wives' expectations as to who should initiate sex, but inconsistent with many husbands' preferences that initiation be equally shared.

Role enactment is inconsistent with normative expectations of men, in that behavior is substantially more husband-oriented than normative expectations would suggest. These findings seem important in that the sexual area is often one of minimal communication between spouses. It seems that husbands especially would desire greater participation in sexual activity on the part of their wives. Wives, on the other hand, seem satisfied to let husbands carry out sexual role responsibilities. Another possible explanation is that wives view sex as being less important to them or something they would frequently prefer to avoid. It is possible that this differential is the cause of many feelings of dissatisfaction between spouses regarding marital sexual activity. These data (Table 6.2) indicate a differential response of men and women when asked how they react when the spouse desires sex while they do not.

In most cases, spouses usually participate when the other spouse desires sex even though they themselves may not desire it at the time. *Husbands are more likely to engage in sexual activity when desired by wives than are wives when husbands desire sexual activity.* Ten percent of the husbands frequently do not respond, but this is true of thirty percent of the wives. Also a full fourth of the wives say they never desire sex when their husband does not.

Table 6.2.

BEHAVIOR OF SPOUSE WHO DOES NOT DESIRE SEX
WHEN OTHER SPOUSE DESIRES SEX
(by sex of respondent; in percentages)

ACTION OF SPOUSE NOT DESIRING SEX	HUSBAND'S REPORT		WIFE'S REPORT	
	Wife Desires Sex When Husband Does Not	Husband Desires Sex When Wife Does Not	Wife Desires Sex When Husband Does Not	Husband Desires Sex When Wife Does Not
Never Participates	1.5	2.0	1.5	2.0
Occasionally Participates	9.8	27.5	6.9	10.3
Usually Participates	42.4	53.9	37.9	65.0
Always Participates	22.0	10.3	28.1	19.2
This Never Happens	24.4	6.4	25.6	3.5
TOTAL	100.1	100.1	100.0	100.0
TOTAL (N)	205	204	203	203

These data suggest that wives are less interested in sexual activity
than are husbands. They are less likely to initiate sexual activity
than would be desired by husbands and they are more likely to
refuse to engage in sexual activity when husbands desire it than are
husbands when wives desire it.

EVALUATION OF SEXUAL ROLE

ENJOYMENT OF SEXUAL ACTIVITY

Wives were asked how often they enjoyed sexual activity and
how often they felt their husbands enjoyed it. While there is little
doubt that both spouses enjoy their sexual activity (over ninety
percent always or usually enjoy it), there are obvious relative
differences.

The findings reflect a greater enjoyment by husbands than by
wives. Thirty-four percent of the wives compared to sixty-eight
percent of the husbands always enjoy sex. It should be emphasized
that husband's enjoyment is reported by the wife and her perception may not always be accurate. Comparable data on this
question were not gathered.

IMPORTANCE OF SEXUAL ACTIVITY

Approximately seventy-three percent of the wives and eighty-five percent of the husbands indicated that sex is extremely or quite important to them. While sex is important to both spouses, more husbands place a higher value on sex than do wives. This is consistent with the findings related to other aspects of the role. This difference in importance is further exemplified when we look at the perceptions of each spouse as to the importance of sex to the other spouse. In viewing the overall distribution, there is a tendency for husbands to perceive that sex is less important to their wives than is indicated by the wives' responses. Only fifty-five percent of the husbands believed it to be extremely or quite important to their wives. These differences provide some additional support for the conviction that husbands are more sex-oriented than wives. Perhaps of more importance is the consistency of this difference throughout the analysis. It also lends support to several other studies that suggest similar conclusions (Blood and Wolfe, 1960; Komarovsky, 1963; Clark and Wallin, 1965).

FREQUENCY OF SEXUAL DESIRE

While desire for sex may not be a direct indicator of the performance of the sexual role, it can be used as an indirect measure in that mutual desire on the part of spouses is likely to be a factor in role performance. Our findings show a close similarity in perceptions of spouses as to the relative sexual desire for each respondent, but a broad gap in the frequency desired by husbands and wives.

Thirty-seven percent of the husbands report that they desire sex much more frequently than their wives, while only two percent report that their wives much more frequently desire sex. Wives agree very closely, but even fewer wives (one percent) report they much more frequently desired sex. The differences are maintained if those who "somewhat more frequently" desire sex are added. This brings the proportion of the husbands to seventy-nine percent compared to eight percent of the wives with a preference for more frequent sex. Not too many spouses report exactly the same actual as desired frequency of intercourse—thirteen percent of husbands and twenty percent of wives (Table 6.3). Thus a majority of husbands but only a tiny minority of wives report a deficit in the frequency of sexual experience. Perhaps it should be recalled, however, that a majority of wives sometimes do not enjoy sex. It might be said they experience a deficit in sexual enjoyment while husbands experience a deficit in frequency.

Table 6.3.

SPOUSE WHO DESIRES SEX MORE FREQUENTLY
(by sex of respondent; in percentages)

DESIRE	HUSBAND'S REPORT	WIFE'S REPORT
Husband Much More Frequently	37.2	34.6
Husband Somewhat More Frequently	41.6	38.1
Husband and Wife the Same	13.0	20.0
Wife Somewhat More Frequently	6.8	6.3
Wife Much More Frequently	1.5	1.0
TOTAL	100.1	100.0
TOTAL (N)	207	205

ROLE STRAIN IN SEXUAL INTERCOURSE

Any set of responsibilities accepted by a group produces feelings on the part of some members that their role enactment is not, or at least sometimes is not, adequate to the role. A sizable proportion of these younger middle-aged spouses report this feeling with respect to their sexual role enactment (wives, thirty-five; and husbands, twenty-two percent) report worrying frequently or "once in a while." On the other hand, over half the wives and two-thirds of the husbands are pleased with the quality of their participation. We have seen above that a sizable proportion of women usually do not respond to the unilateral sexual interests of their spouses, while many husbands do not, at times, stimulate a pleasurable response in their wives during intercourse. Apparently failure to participate is more clearly a role deficiency than the type of sexual encounter, since more wives than husbands feel guilty about their sexual role.

SUBCULTURAL DIFFERENCES

Social class analysis reveals some expected and some unexpected differences. Among the latter is that higher-middle-class husbands are more likely to express a belief that the husband should be the one to initiate sexual activity. This is inconsistent with equalitarian ideologies usually attributed to middle-class men. However, it seems congruent with the greater power usually reported for upper-middle-class husbands. Consistent with this normative position is the reported behavior that a higher proportion of middle-class men are the ones that initiate intercourse. Also, men who work long hours are more likely to regard sex as very important. This implies that long working hours do not reduce sexual potency in men. Wives of men who work longer hours are also more likely to report that their husbands enjoy sex. One might speculate that the greater involvement in an occupation creates greater need for the emotional and physical pleasures of sex, or perhaps such men have a greater supply of physical and psychic energy. Such questions are intriguing, but go beyond the scope of the present analysis.

There appears to be a curvilinear relationship between the wife's education and enjoyment of sex, with an increase in sexual satisfaction up through "some college" but with a major drop-off for women college graduates. It may be the latter have higher sexual expectations, or other related variables may be involved. A previous relationship may be relevant—that a higher proportion of men married to college graduates report strain in the therapeutic role (Chapter 7). Also, related is the greater difference in sexual desires of men with increased education level.

Concerning extramarital sexual intercourse, upper-middle-class husbands are less likely to be completely opposed. This can be related to the Kinsey findings (1948) that a higher proportion of upper-middle-class men have extramarital sexual relationships.

RELIGIOUS VARIATION

Religious differences are relatively,[1] perhaps surprisingly, few. Fundamentalist Protestant husbands are a little more likely to initiate sexual activity and Fundamentalist and Catholic wives more likely to participate sexually when they do not desire intercourse. The latter are also more likely to completely condemn extramarital intercourse. No differences in sexual satisfaction are reported.

SITUATIONAL VARIATION

Few situational differences were found. Women with larger families were more likely to report sexual satisfaction. Younger wives were more likely to initiate intercourse than older ones. We have noted that men who worked longer hours valued and enjoyed sex more, but the employment status of the wife was unrelated to any sexual norms, behavior, stress, or satisfaction.

In sum, if our sample is representative, no revolutionary change in marital sexual behavior seems to have occurred among typical American couples during the past few decades. At the time the data were gathered, most of the wives viewed sex as essentially a marital activity which should be initiated primarily by the husband. Husbands, however, desired to see more female initiative in sexual intercourse. In light of the advocacy of changing ideologies toward sexual behavior, repeated studies seem imperative to monitor changing sexual behavior and values among married as well as single Americans.

Chapter 7

THE THERAPEUTIC ROLE

F. Ivan Nye

We took the position in Chapter 1 that not only do old roles decline and disappear from the social structure, but new ones appear. We view the therapeutic role as one that is in the process of being incorporated into the social structure.

RELATIONSHIP TO PREVIOUS CONCEPTUALIZATION

Our present conceptualization substantively bears considerable resemblance to Blood and Wolfe's mental hygiene function. However, we prefer to conceptualize roles in terms of the behavior involved rather than the product or result of the behavior. The behavior, as we present it, is therapeutic in assisting the spouse to cope with and, hopefully, dispose of the problem with which he is confronted. The therapeutic role is broader in scope than Blood and Wolfe's mental hygiene role in that the latter deals only with problems external to the pair. Some problems originate in the interaction between spouses, their feelings toward each other, and the meanings that each attaches to the actions or attitudes of the other. The therapeutic role of the spouse includes these interspousal problems and meanings as well as with those that involve other family members or non-family individuals or groups. However, our thinking is close to Blood and Wolfe's, where they write,

Psychotherapy is not for everyone, nor forever. Yet it provides an analogy for the help which everyone needs with ordinary emotional problems. People need opportunities for catharsis, for ventilating their feelings, for help in interpreting their difficulties, for emotional support and encouragement. Where can such lifetime therapy-as-needed be found better than in marriage [1960: 180]?

To be human and to be alive is to have problems. If the problems are sufficiently severe, and if one has the necessary financial resources, they are likely to be taken to a professional therapist—provided the society is sufficiently differentiated to provide such specialized services. However, even in such societies, only a tiny fraction of problems is taken to professionals. Most are shared with spouses, parents, or friends, or the individual struggles with them alone. That spouses are frequently utilized was shown by Blood and Wolfe in their Detroit study, in that about half of the wives always or usually shared their bad experiences with their husbands. Only about one-quarter seldom or never utilized the husband in this way. In response, about fifty percent of the husbands took some positive action to assist with the problem, while an additional eighteen percent passively listened (Blood and Wolfe, 1960: 206). If one considers such listening as a contribution, about eighty percent of the husbands in their sample in whom wives confide assist in problem-solving to some extent. It should be noted, however, that this is eighty percent of those in whom wives confide rather than eighty percent of all husbands in the sample.

From the above, it is evident that a role bearing many similarities to the therapeutic role (and actually utilizing that term to describe the behavior) was evident to some sociologists as early as 1955 (Parsons and Bales, 1955) and that considerable spousal behavior consonant with the concept was measured by Blood and Wolfe. The interim period has disclosed no appreciable development of the concept either as a mental hygiene or a therapeutic role.

Komarovsky deals with some substantive parts of the role in analyzing how spouses deal with depression or "bad moods." In her sample of blue-collar marriages, she found that about half get some help from talking with others, while the balance utilize other activity as a diversion from the problem, or do nothing at all to deal with the emotional problem. Of those who turn to people for help with their moods, about half (one-fourth of the total sample) get more help from the spouse than from any other source. The wife is a particularly important source for the better-educated husbands—thirty percent list her as the most valuable aide in dealing with emotional problems (Komarovsky, 1962: 187). Husbands with little education find difficulty in communicating their problems and receiving aid from interaction either with wife or others. Komarovsky does mention the term therapeutic: "The less-educated husbands, who do not find emotional relief in social interaction, are less able to avail themselves of the therapeutic function of marriage and to fulfill it for their wives" (Komarovsky, 1962: 190). However, she does not develop the concept or utilize it extensively. Her line of analysis deals more extensively with communication and problem-sharing than with problem-solving per se.

Goode gives incidental attention to some portions of the therapeutic role in discussing changes from extended to conjugal family organization:

> Since the larger kin group can no longer be counted on for emotional sustenance, and since the marriage is based on mutual attraction, the small marital unit is the main place where the emotional input-output balance of the individual husband and wife is maintained, where their psychic wounds can be solved or healed. At least there is no other place where they can go [Goode, 1963: 9].

Gurin, Veroff and Feld, in a nationwide mental health study, asked respondents how they handled worries and periods of depression. Some thirty percent reported that they went to other people with their worries, and about twenty-five percent sought similar help with periods of depression. (Since they tabulated only the first-mentioned source of help, presumably the total proportion seeking help from this source is considerably higher than those figures.) Of those seeking help from others, fifty-six percent mentioned spouse as first source of help with worries, but only seventeen percent as first resource for periods of unhappiness. Their conceptualization of problems either as a worry or a period of depression is somewhat more restricted than utilized by Komarovsky or as we conceptualize it, so direct comparison between their data and ours cannot be made. However, in general, they see problem-solving as a day-to-day, if not hour-to-hour, condition of humanity and find spouses frequently are asked for help and respond to such requests (Gurin et al., 1960: ch. 12).

Some substantive aspects of the therapeutic role are described for the wives of a specialized occupational group, executives, by Whyte. He has written,

Above all, wives emphasize, they have to be good listeners. They describe the job somewhat wryly. They *must* be "sounding boards," "refueling stations," "wailing walls." But they speak without resentment. Nurturing the male ego, they seem to feel, is not only a pretty good fulfillment of their own ego but a form of therapy made *increasingly necessary*, by the corporation way of life. Management psychologists couldn't agree more. "Most top executives are very lonely people," as one puts it. "The greatest thing a man's wife can do is let him unburden the worries he can't confess to in the office" [Whyte, 1952: 178; italics added] .

It is evident that Whyte is acutely aware of the needs of some husbands, notably executives, for some types of therapeutic role enactment from their wives. It is equally clear that he does not see such wives enacting the whole range of problem-solving which we term the therapeutic role. Nor does one sense any reciprocity in the husband enacting a therapeutic role for the wife. In this latter respect, his discussion is similar to that of Parons, Zelditch, and their students, who have proposed a division of labor with respect to the substantive content of this role, viewing it as the responsibility of wife and mother.

RELATIONSHIP TO EXPRESSIVE ROLE

It is clear from the preceding discussion that others, notably Blood and Wolfe (but not limited to them), have been thinking about and measuring behavior which we term the *therapeutic role*. However, a related concept has had wide currency during the same period—that of an *expressive role*. Zelditch used the term, along with *instrumental role* in an essay in 1955, taking both from behavior in small group research. Zelditch did not offer a precise definition, but made a number of statements about the role, as it is performed both in small group research and in family behavior. Later, in testing the idea that the instrumental role is usually delegated to the male, the expressive to the female, he develops a set of indicators for both roles. From these, it is possible to get an approximation of the content of the expressive role. He states,

> Ego will be considered the expressive leader of the nuclear family if . . . Ego is the mediator, conciliator, of the family; Ego soothes over disputes, resolves hostilities in the family. Ego is affectionate, solicitous, warm, emotional to the children of the family; Ego is the comforter, the consoler, is relatively indulgent, relatively unpunishing [Zelditch, 1955: 318].

It can be seen that two analytically separate ideas compose the expressive role. The term itself means only to communicate, to express. As such, it could as well communicate negative and hostile as affectionate and supportive content. However, the indicators listed above to be used to evaluate role behavior are all positive. In the literature, the two have been blended so that expressive has come to mean the communication of positive emotions and behavior encouraging such emotions among other family members. Such behavior is not limited to problems requiring it. The assumption apparently has been that the need for such behavior is always present in the family group and that the need always exceeds the amount of expressive behavior available.

There is some common content in the expressive and therapeutic roles. Problem-solving frequently involves feelings of insecurity, lack of appreciation or love. If so, the therapeutic role player may be able to supply some of the needed emotional support. Certainly such emotional content is relevant to much problem-solving. However, the therapeutic role includes a much broader range of content. Listening and giving the family member an opportunity to verbalize, acting as a "sounding board" for the ideas or reactions of the other, supplying additional information, concepts, or insights and taking concrete actions in sharing the solution of the problem are all involved. Thus, the concept encompasses a considerably broader range of responsibilities and actions than the expressive role.

Another difference of some importance involves a basic assumption of the two roles. The therapeutic role is problem-focused. For example, the role player does not offer love and reassurance unless he or she perceives the other family member as providing definite indications of feeling rejected or insecure. It assumes most people most of the time feel sufficiently secure and accepted so that they have no need for a continuous input from another family member. The assumptions surrounding the expressive role seem to be that such needs are continuous and pressing.

Finally, needs for emotional support in the expressive role seem to be limited to the husband and the children, since the wife-mother is seen as enacting the role. The assumption seems to be that adult tensions originate in the extramural environment, but children's may arise within the family. No such assumptions are made about the therapeutic role. The assumption was made by Blood and Wolfe that wives and mothers have problems too and that at least their husbands enact the therapeutic role (Blood and Wolfe, 1960).

RELATIONSHIP TO SOCIOEMOTIONAL ROLE

Levinger has drawn from the same small group research to describe a family role but utilizes the somewhat more descriptive term socioemotional role. This deemphasizes the communication dimension of the role and emphasizes the substantive aspects, relationships, and emotional properties of the family. Levinger also challenged the notion that task roles fall in the male and socioemotional in the female domain. Both are task specialists and socioemotional specialists. He further proposed that socioemotional behavior in the pair relationship must be reciprocal (Levinger, 1964).

More recently Litwak (1970: 361-362) also leveled a strong criticism against the notion of the separation of instrumental and socioemotional behavior. He writes,

It has been maintained that for small groups such as families to continue to exist, two essential functions must be carried out which require different leaders. The instrumental leader insures that the group deals in an effective way with its goals. The socio-emotional leader insures that group cohesion is continually stressed. These two functions generally must be in the hands of two different people because they frequently stress contradictory elements. . . . This line of reasoning makes several major assumptions which in my view are incorrect. It assumes that the wife does not have tensions which are equal to the husband's. For instance, it would accordingly be assumed that the following events do not produce tensions for the wife equal to any felt by the husband in his life experiences: birth of a child; children leaving home; illness of children; adjustment to new neighborhoods; illness, etc. If the wife does have great anxieties, there is no ideal person (according to this ideal sex-linked division concept) who can provide her succour. In my opinion it is incorrect to say that the wife does not have anxieties that are equal [to] if not greater than the man's. As a consequence the division of labor advocated would not in principle meet the needs of the family to alleviate tensions. . . .

It is difficult to know how a family (with its multiplicity of tasks and limited membership) would survive even in principle if the husband were to be responsible for all the instrumental tasks and the wife for only the tension management ones. The division of labor into separate task and socio-emotional leaders which makes sense in a single-task experimental group becomes unmanageable if applied in blind fashion to a multitasked two-person primary group [Litwak, 1970: 361-362].

The present formulation of the therapeutic role differs substantially from Levinger's conceptualization of the socioemotional role. It is less inclusive in that it does not include all the social relationships among family members—only those behaviors which are involved in problem-solving. It is much more inclusive in that it also deals with problems whose origin is outside the family group and that it includes a number of activities and behaviors in addition to providing emotional support to other family members.

In short, there is some overlap in the content of expressive, socioemotional, and therapeutic role concepts. All require communication between individuals and all include, either as the principal or some lesser content, emotional reassurance and support, but as we have noted above, there is much included in the therapeutic role that is not conceptualized in others and there is some content in the socioemotional not included in the therapeutic. Too, there are some important differences in assumptions about the nature of human needs and concerning who enacts the role.

The common substantive elements between our conceptualization and that of Blood and Wolfe is extensive. The largest differences are not in the behavior included but in the conceptual identification. They employ the term "mental health function in marriage." Within this function they identify and describe therapeutic behavior, whereas we prefer to identify the role from the substantive content—therapy. We share with Blood and Wolfe the assumption that it meets needs which are presumably similar in frequency and urgency for men and women, and both spouses enact the role for each other and for their children. Since we have data from both husbands and wives, this assumption will be put to a rigorous test.

NORMATIVE DEFINITION

From sociological and counseling literature, four positive responses to a problem were found: (1) listens to the problem, (2) sympathizes, (3) gives reassurance and affection, (4) offers help in solving the problem. From the literature, we were able to find only two types of proscribed role behavior: (1) reacts with criticism of the person confiding the problem, and (2) discloses confidences to third parties. However, therapists attending the 1973 World Congress on Mental Health and those attending the Third Annual Family Research Conference at Provo, Utah, suggested a third: "takes over" and imposes one's own solutions on the confider.

We treat the therapeutic role as a hypothesis. The hypothesis that such a role exists is subjected to two tests: the beliefs of respondents that spouses have a duty to perform the role and evidence that some type of sanction is provided for nonperformance of the prescriptions and against behavior violating the proscriptions.

To test for the normative component of the role, respondents were given the following item:

Some people feel it is not part of a wife's (husband's) duty to help her
husband (his wife) with personal problems, others feel it is a duty. What
are your feelings?

The beliefs of the respondents concerning one's duty to play a
therapeutic role, actual role behavior of each sex, and, finally,
whether they disapprove of spouses who refuse to enact the role
are shown in Figure 7.1.

As stated above, the therapeutic role is treated as a hypothesis;
that is, that the role probably exists in American society but that
previous evidence was not sufficiently strong to make a positive
assertion of the existence of the role (Nye, 1974). In order to
accept this hypothesis, it is necessary to show that a majority of
spouses define the role normatively—that spouses have a duty to
enact it and, if they fail, that sanctions at least in the form of
disapproval should result.

Over sixty percent of both husbands and wives indicate that
their sex has a duty to enact the role, with most of the remaining
affirming the desirability of such role enactment. Likewise, over
three-fifths indicate strong disapproval of a member of their own
sex who refuses to assist the spouse with a problem. The above
offer substantial evidence that both men and women see problem-
solving as a duty. However, norms frequently include proscriptions
as well as prescriptions. Initially, we identified two: (1) revealing
sensitive behavior to people outside the family, and (2) responding
to a spouse's problem with criticism for having become involved in
the problem or for failing to handle it competently. Concerning
the first of these, a question was asked how the respondent would
react to a spouse who revealed information to a friend about
family financial problems, sex, problems with children, and problems with in-laws.

Both husbands and wives disapproved of revealing information
about any of these topics to outsiders. At least sixty percent of
women and seventy percent of men took this position. However,
verbal sanctions were stronger for some of these matters than for
others. Over seventy percent of both sexes *strongly* disapproved
revealing sexual problems to outsiders, and about ninety percent
of both disapproved such behavior. Fewest disapprove of sharing

Table 7.1.

FREQUENCY WITH WHICH RESPONDENTS UTILIZED FAMILY AND NONFAMILY PERSONS
FOR THERAPEUTIC PURPOSES (in percentages)

THERAPEUTIC ROLE ENACTOR	FREQUENTLY		OCCASIONALLY		SELDOM		NEVER		TOTAL	
	Husband	Wife	Husband	Wife	Husband	Wife	Husband	Wife	Husband	Wife
Spouse	72	71	22	22	6	6	1	2	101	101
Father	2	1	16	16	34	20	49	63	101	100
Mother	1	7	18	29	42	38	39	26	100	100
Sister	0	7	5	26	33	20	62	46	100	99
Brother	2	2	12	8	31	27	55	62	100	99
Other Family	1	2	7	18	22	23	70	58	100	101
Friend-Same Sex	3	14	27	34	33	34	37	19	100	101
Friend-Other Sex	0	1	8	5	28	19	64	75	100	100
Neighbor	1	2	5	15	25	23	70	61	101	101
Professional Counselor	1	1	4	4	8	7	88	89	101	101
Clergyman	1	2	12	9	19	16	68	73	100	100
Other	1	1	2	6	6	3	91	91	100	101

No one—Husband = 8%; Wife = 3%.

the problems of one's children with outsiders, but even in this less sensitive area, about half would disapprove. Responding to a confidance with criticism was disapproved by over eighty-five percent of each sex.

Role enactment corresponds approximately to normative prescriptions for the role. It may be a coincidence, but sixty-one percent of wives feel it is their spouse's duty, sixty-three percent would strongly disapprove if he or she did not enact it, and sixty-three percent of the husbands *do* enact the role actively. The correspondence is less precise for women. Sixty-nine percent of their husbands see it as a duty, the same proportion would strongly disapprove of a spouse who refused to enact the role, but even more, eighty percent of the wives usually do enact it. Put another way, wives are a little more responsive in their behavior than husbands. The number of men who see it as a duty and strongly disapprove of a failure to respond do enact the role, but in addition to such wives, some wives who only see it as preferable also usually actively enact it.

Of those who usually actively enact the role women appear also to do so in somewhat different ways. Sixty-seven percent of women, compared to sixty-three percent of men, usually try to help solve the problem. About the same proportion of each sex—fifty-six percent of women, fifty-five percent of men—usually give reassurance and affection, but forty-two percent of women while only twenty-eight percent of men usually respond with sympathy. Therefore, it appears that a smaller proportion of women are failing—if we consider a passive or negative reaction failure—in the enactment of the role. About four in five women seem minimally adequate but only a little more than three in five men in this sample reached that level. Perhaps this is the reason that large numbers of women frequently take their problems to female relatives and friends (Table 7.1).

THE ENACTMENT OF THE THERAPEUTIC ROLE

As a family member is faced with a problem, several alternatives may be available. If a person is married, he or she may share the problem with the spouse. If the spouse is not willing or considered competent, the problem may be taken outside the nuclear family to a parent or sibling. Finally, it may be taken outside the boundaries of kinship to a friend or professional counselor.

To determine who enacts the therapeutic role, each spouse in the sample was asked, "Who do you talk to about your problems?" and was presented with a list of family members and persons outside the family including friends, neighbors, professional counselors, and the clergy. In Table 7.1, the distribution of responses was shown. Respondents were not limited to a single response, so one could indicate that one discussed problems with the spouse, other members of the family and with nonmembers, if this was one's mode of dealing with them, or one could indicate that he or she usually discussed them with no one.

The results leave no doubt of the dominant place of the spouse in enacting the therapeutic role, since over seventy percent of both sexes report frequent sharing of problems with the spouse. It also clearly establishes the husband as well as the wife as a therapeutic agent, and strongly challenges the Parsons-Zelditch proposition that this function is allocated primarily to the wife. Rather, it provides strong support for Litwak's contention that the wife encounters as many frustrations and problems as does the husband.

It is also evident that wives more frequently than husbands utilize extended family and nonfamily persons in dealing with their problems. There is little difference in their interaction with their fathers and brothers—neither sex confides extensively in them—but wives confide with some frequency in their mothers, sisters, and especially with friends of their own sex. Neither sex extensively uses the clergy or professional counselors.

These data do not establish that wives have more problems or more serious problems than do husbands (a check of our data on role and relationship problems failed to substantiate this), but they do show that wives are more likely to discuss problems with someone—if not the husband then with a female relative or friend. Only three percent report that they usually talk to no one, compared to more than double that figure for men.

ROLE COMPETENCE

Spouses vary in role competence from those viewed as superlative role players to those who refuse to enact a role at all, or as in the case of the therapeutic role, may actually aggravate the problem by negative and hostile behavior. Competence may be viewed in relationship to perfect role performance, minimal role enactment, or a standard believed prevalent in one's reference groups. This evaluative question was phrased in terms of general criteria, as follows: "How well do you feel you do at helping your wife (husband) with personal problems? How well do you feel your wife (husband) does at helping you?"

It appears that about half of the spouses feel satisfied with their own role performance, in indicating they do quite or extremely well. Wives, however, give the more conservative evaluation both of their own competence and of their husbands'. Almost three-fourths of husbands consider wives competent, compared to less than half of wives who evaluate themselves that favorably. Men tend to be more modest in evaluating themselves in this role. Half regard themselves as competent, and their wives agree with this more modest evaluation. As a category, wives tend to rate themselves and husbands at about the same level of competence. However, the men's rating agrees better with other data which finds a smaller proportion of women than men who enact only passive or negative role-playing.

At the incompetent end of the continuum, wives again take a more pessimistic view of both their own and their husbands' role enactment. Seventeen percent feel their husbands are poor role players or don't try at all, while twelve percent feel the same way about their own performance. Here, husbands' self-evaluation is similar to wives' self-evaluation, but fewer men feel they are failures than women feel they are.

We have suggested that active, positive role enactment is more competent than passive listening or reacting negatively. While this appears plausible, data are available to test it. It appears that the above preliminary judgment was correct. Spouses who usually offer help, reassurance, and affection or sympathy are in most instances evaluated by their spouses as competent; those who listen only, criticize, or show that they do not want to listen are in most instances evaluated as not competent.

However, by no means all of the spouses who do not want to be bothered by their mate's problems or those who usually respond with criticism view *themselves* as incompetent. Of those who usually make one of these responses, 37.5 percent of the men stated that they considered themselves competent, and thirteen percent of the women in those two categories held similar opinions. These data permit two generalizations: (1) most spouses who respond actively and positively to their spouse's problems consider themselves competent in helping solve problems, and (2) an appreciable minority who react negatively to their spouse's problems view this as appropriate and helpful. However, in most instances their spouses do not concur. The data further suggest that women as a sex hold higher standards for enactment of the role and a larger proportion are good role players. More exactly, they number a smaller proportion who fail to enact the role or do so negatively.

INDENTIFICATION WITH ROLE

It is characteristic of role that occupants of a position have limited choices in whether or not they will enact the role. Choices usually exist in how one will enact it, but if one occupies a position he or she is under pressure to enact the roles in the position at a level acceptable to the society or at least to the reference groups. Therefore, role players are volunteers in only a limited sense that they may have a choice in deciding not to occupy a position. Since role choices are limited, it seemed well to know how role players feel about their roles. With respect to the therapeutic role, data were gathered on role players' feelings: whether or not they liked the role. The question was phrased, "How do you feel about helping your husband (wife) with his (her) problems? (Always want to help, usually want to help, no feelings one way or the other, usually don't want to help, never want to help.)" Responses to this general question were generally affirmative. About half of each sex—wives, fifty-six percent; husbands, forty-four percent—indicated that they always want to help. Perhaps it is no coincidence that this is about the proportion rated competent role players by their spouses. Also, the higher proportion of wives who are, presumably, always willing to assist agrees with the data analyzed above which show more wives than husbands competent in this role. Most of the remaining spouses— forty-three percent of wives and fifty-four percent of husbands— indicate they usually want to help. However, this attitude seems usually not translated into action by an appreciable number of wives and a larger number of husbands (Figure 7.1). Attitude research has shown this gap between attitude and behavior is not unusual. Fatigue, other duties, lack of confidence in one's ability to do so or limitations on the spouse's ability to receive and use the type of help proffered might be among the reasons for non-activity. In addition, we have seen that some types of therapeutic response such as responding with criticism or listening only are interpreted by some of the role players as adequate responses even though the spouse and the researcher would not agree.

Figure 7.1

**NORMATIVE DEFINITION, ROLE ENACTMENT AND SANCTIONS TO
ENFORCE THE THERAPEUTIC ROLE**

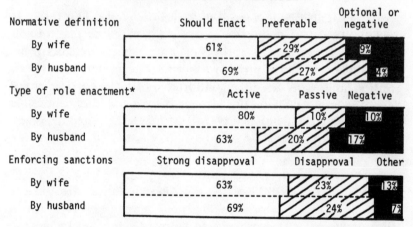

*Passive = Listening only; negative = dislikes listening or responds with criticism; Active = Sympathizes, gives affection and reassurance and/or tries to solve problem

THERAPEUTIC ROLE AS VALUE

The assumption is made that any set of responsibilities normatively defined with sanctions to enforce or prohibit the relevant behavior is paralleled by a set of values which give meaning to the role. To determine the distribution and intensity of values on the therapeutic role, respondents were asked: "How important is it to you (to your wife or husband) to have someone with whom to share problems?"

A majority of husbands and wives consider the therapeutic role of some importance to both themselves and their spouse, yet a substantial number do not, about forty percent of the husbands and thirty percent of the wives. This value by such a substantial minority suggests that the query may not have been worded adequately. If it had been worded "help with your problem" instead of "share your problems" the value response likely would have been a little stronger and more fully congruent with the responses to the normative and sanction items. In this sample, both sexes agree that therapeutic services are important *to more wives than husbands,* although the differences are not statistically significant.

STRAIN IN THE THERAPEUTIC ROLE

Just as occupants of a position have little choice in whether to enact the roles of the position, there is no assurance that the role player can enact it at a level of competency which meets his or her own standards or those of the spouse and reference groups.

Many spouses are less than comfortable with their enactment of the therapeutic role. One in five reports frequent worry about her (his) performance, and nearly half (forty-eight percent) worry frequently or occasionally.

THE SOCIAL DISTRIBUTION OF THERAPEUTIC ROLE BEHAVIOR

It is believed that new cultural forms do not develop at the same rate in all parts of a complex society. Because of advanced education which exposes youth to new ideas and behavioral alternatives, it is often expected that social change will occur in the middle class first. Likewise it is sometimes assumed that members of some of the "liberal" Protestant denominations are likely to change their attitudes and behavior more readily than some of the more conservative religious groups. Also, some specific situations might tend to increase the need for therapy or affect the availability of the spouse for providing it. The presence of a disabled person or an exceptional number of children is an example of the type of situation which might increase the need; the full-time employment of the wife or "moonlighting" on a second job by the husband are considered to be situations in which a spouse might have inadequate time or energy to enact the role.

With respect to the above, we think of social class and religious organizations as affecting the role by virtue of subcultural differences—in the normative beliefs or one's duty or absence of it; the latter as situational variables in which other duties and activities differentially impinge on the time and energy resources of the spouse, affecting availability and performance as a therapist.

SOCIAL CLASS

Present data suggest that sharing one's problems with one's spouse or the reaction of the spouse to the problem is not, to any extent, class-related. Men in the highest and lowest class categories share problems about equally with wives. There is no evidence that members of liberal churches are more likely to obtain therapeutic help from the spouse, either, therefore the expectation that the role might emerge differentially by subculture is not supported. Role enactment does not differ much by the subcultures sampled. (Data are not at this writing available for Black, Native American or Latin American couples.) An interesting but unanticipated class-related finding is that men in business and professional occupations share more problems with associates and other friends, and that women active in church and other community activities do likewise. These men and women do not utilize such additional therapeutic resources as substitutes for interaction with the spouse, but in addition to it.

Wives' behavior in utilizing therapeutic assistance of the husband is not class-related or related to religious affiliation, but lower-class women are more likely to take problems to relatives *also* than are middle-class women.

We had anticipated that middle-class spouses would be more competent in the therapeutic role and would evaluate themselves as being more competent, but the data do not support that expectation. The relationship of role strain to socioeconomic variables is a little surprising. It is highest for men in low blue-collar occupations and for men with college and graduate education. Difference variables must be involved with the two opposite groups. Strain among highly educated men may be explained by the high expectations of highly educated wives. Of college men married to women who were college graduates, seventy percent reported strain compared to forty percent of those married to women with less education. The same explanation could hardly serve for men in lower blue-collar occupations. It may be that these men feel strain because their lack of competence in the provider role gives them limited resources to commit to their wives and children—in short, this limited cómpetence may be the source of many of the problems; or a possible alternative may be that this category of men lacks communication skills.

College-educated women show no disproportionate role strain; in fact, for women there is no relationship between education and role strain. However, women active in no organizations and those working in unskilled occupations do show more strain. This suggests that, for women, the lack of communication skills may be the crucial variable.

Value placed on the therapeutic role varies little by social class, yet one variation in the male sample is suggestive. It is the lower blue-collar men who are more likely to highly value having a person with whom to share their problems. This suggests that the experiences of inadequately enacting or failing to enact the provider role may be more devastating for men than the obvious stresses in role performance in professional and executive positions.

The value placed on the therapeutic role by women does not vary by their education, family income, or husband's occupation, but it does by a related variable—the number of organizations in which they are active. Sixty-five percent of the women active in four or more organizations value it highly compared to only thirty-six percent who are active in no or one organization. A similar and rather obviously related finding is that, of women regularly attending church, sixty-two percent value the role while of those never attending, only twenty-three percent value it. These data suggest that extensive social interaction in the relatively unstructured domain of voluntary organizations creates a need for confidantes. However, gainfully employed women do not communicate a greater need; in fact, the small difference suggests a lesser need for confidantes than has the full-time housewife.

OVEREMPLOYMENT

Two groups of spouses have unusual demands on their time—the fully employed wife and the "moonlighting" husband who works more than forty-eight hours weekly. The literature speculates that these will tend to lack the time and energy to help solve their spouse's problems. Some women have given this as a reason for not taking gainful employment. However, no differences that are related to the number of hours a person is employed are found in enacting the therapeutic role. Time does not appear to be a critical variable in enacting the therapeutic role. Nor is there any difference in the effectiveness of their role enactment, nor in reported role strain. All this suggests a conclusion that neither sex, ordinarily, need limit the hours worked because of a concern that longer hours would interfere with this role.

FAMILY COMPOSITION

Women with more children or with a disabled person in the home are more likely to share problems with their spouses. Those with large families also confide more with kin.

DISCUSSION

The normative, sanction and behavioral data confirm the hypothesis of a therapeutic role—one not confined to the middle class or any other narrow segment of families. However, an appreciable minority of spouses do not view it as a duty or enact it in any positive way. Thus, the role does not appear to be as fully crystalized as some of the traditional family roles. Initial data suggest appreciable sex differences—not only that more women enact the role well, but also that they value it highly. Thus, there appears to be a disjunction between the "supply" and the "demand." More women enact the role positively than think it is their duty to do so. In order to meet their needs, women use nonnuclear family sources more than do men.

It is interesting to speculate why a larger proportion of women are prepared to enact the role and to do so in a positive sense. This may be a way that wives obtain information concerning their husbands' jobs and job-related activities, and, through enacting the role, obtain a more meaningful part in decisions about it. Whether the husband retains employment and advances to better-paid positions and to positions with more security and/or prestige is of direct concern to the wife. Husbands may not feel an equal interest and concern about wives' problems in women's clubs or with child care. Even wives' jobs may be of less concern because they contribute a smaller fraction of family income. Many wives want husbands to talk more to them but many men want the women to talk less.

Value placed on the role, identification with it, and role strain in it are less than for most family roles, but this may involve a lack of recognition of its importance for the individual's mental health and sense of well-being, or its importance for the viability of marriage. Its relationship to satisfaction in marriage is greater than for most of the other family roles (see Chapter 11).

Chapter 8

THE RECREATIONAL ROLE

John Carlson

One of the many changes in American society during the past several years has been the changing relationship between work and leisure. While the factors affecting this change are too numerous and complex to mention here, the results have been documented by many (Clawson, 1964; Davis, 1970). Longer paid vacations, shorter work weeks, and more three-day weekends provide increased time for recreational activities. Higher standards of living along with more discretionary income provide additional incentives to engage in a wider variety of recreational activities. Such changes have resulted in a greater than anticipated participation in recreation (especially outdoor recreation) during the past decade or so.

During this period, existing facilities were unable to absorb the increasing demand and previous projections of demand were found to be inaccurate. Thus, numerous studies have been carried out during the past few years focusing on the background characteristics of recreational users in hopes of finding sets of factors useful for predicting one's choice of recreational activities (Burch, 1969; Burdge, 1969; Clarke, 1955). These studies have been less than successful in their objectives. This inability to explain a large proportion of the variance in recreational activities can possibly be traced to two factors: (1) the focus of researchers on the individual as the basic unit in recreation rather than the family, (2) the implicit view that recreational activities exist in a context relatively free of normative constraints. The primary focus of previous research has been on the socio-economic backgrounds of individuals as predicting individual recreational activities. Cunningham and Johannis (1960: 25; italics in original) have emphasized this tendency by stating that

> most of the empirical research which has been reported treats the impact of non-work time on *individual* behavior. Research concerned with the influence of non-work time on family members roles [sic] or the family as a unity of interacting participant role behavior is at a premium.

Though written more than ten years ago, this statement still seems true; there is little research that focuses on the interaction patterns associated with family recreation. This becomes even more important in light of the findings suggesting that most outdoor recreation is engaged in by family units (Burch, 1964b; King, 1968).

It has been suggested above that recreation is often viewed as an individual activity affected by individual characteristics. An alternative hypothesis is that *recreational activities are primarily group activities and recreational choices are made within a framework of group decision-making and reference group norms and values.* This later hypothesis is taken as the framework utilized in this chapter. It is hypothesized that spouses perceive recreation within a normative context. If a set of expectations concerning family recreation exists and is reinforced by negative sanctions for failure to carry out family recreation, then the existence of a family recreation role can be hypothesized.

Numerous writers have attempted to define recreation or leisure (DeGrazia, 1962; Clawson, 1964; Burch and Taves, 1961; Arendt, 1959). The characterization of recreation used in this study will be similar to the limitations and functions of leisure discussed by Dumazedier (1967) in his study of French workers. When respondents were asked to indicate the type of activities in contrast with leisure, the following list resulted:

(1) the job;

(2) supplementary work or occasional odd jobs;

(3) domestic tasks (housework, and the strictly utilitarian aspects of animal care, miscellaneous chores, gardening),

(4) care of the person (bathing and dressing, sleep),

(5) family ritual and ceremonies, social and religious,

(6) obligations (visits, anniversaries, political meetings, church duties), and

(7) necessary study (for study circles, for school or professional examination).

Furthermore, when asked to list the functions of leisure, the responses grouped into three categories: relaxation, entertainment, and personal development (Dumazedier, 1967: 13-14). On the basis of these responses, recreation was defined as "activity—apart from the obligations of work, family, and society—to which the individual turns at will, for either relaxation, diversion or broadening his knowledge and his spontaneous social participation, the free exercise of his creative capacity" (Dumazedier, 1967: 16-17). This definition still seems to present conflicting elements. For example, the free exercise of one's creative capacity seemingly could be as much a part of one's paid occupation as an aspect of recreation or leisure. On the other hand, recreation as used in this study seems to possess aspects of the three elements—relaxation, entertainment, and personal development—found in Dumazedier's study. It should be stressed that certain activities may not fall clearly within the domain of either work or recreation. For example, certain household activities such as sewing, knitting, puttering around, and gardening may only be semi-obligatory and semi-pleasurable; activities such as these might be characterized as semi-recreational activities. Also, activities which may be recreational or semi-recreational for one person may be work for another person. This interrelationship between work and recreation can be made more explicit by referring to Figure 8.1.

Respondents in this study were allowed to define recreation within their own frame of reference in that they were asked to list their most frequent recreational activities with no restrictions

Figure 8.1

THE INTERRELATIONSHIP BETWEEN WORK AND RECREATION

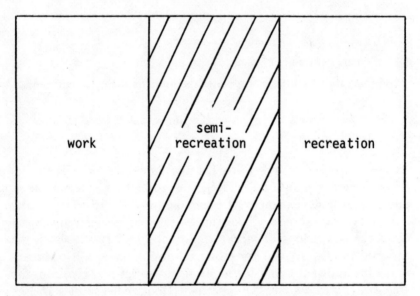

placed on the types of responses. What the individual felt was his recreational activities provided the criteria for defining recreational activities in this study.

RELEVANT RESEARCH AND THE FAMILY RECREATION ROLE

While recreation as a family activity has a place in the sociological literature (for example, Ogburn, 1938), except for Bates (1956) we have not seen it conceptualized as a role. Most studies dealing with recreation in any detail have been descriptive in nature, focusing primarily on the kinds of recreation families engage in and the factors affecting these activities.

Nye (1958) looked at the effects of employment status of mothers on their recreational activities. Based on his findings, two conclusions were drawn: (1) mothers' employment results in a decline in recreation involving social participation outside the family, (2) intra-family and commercial recreation are not appreciably affected by mothers' employment.

Burch (1966) and Harry (1970) have both looked at the effects of family life cycle on recreational choice. Burch found that family life cycle had an effect on the type of family outdoor camping. Harry found that the presence of children had a negative effect on the wife's membership and participation in voluntary associations.

Another area for research in family recreation has focused on its effect on marital satisfaction. Gerson (1960) found a positive correlation between a number of leisure variables and marital satisfaction among college couples. The relationship seemed stronger for husbands than for wives. West and Merriam (1969) also found a positive relationship between family solidarity and outdoor recreation. One difficulty with this type of research is determining a cause-effect relationship. Does engaging in joint recreation cause family solidarity or does family solidarity facilitate joint recreation? Such questions must be dealt with in future studies.

Blood and Wolfe (1960), in their study of Detroit families, dealt with recreation only as it related to marital disagreements. Yet the very fact that recreation ranked high as an area of disagreement indicates that it is more important to families than the literature has suggested. As with the above-mentioned studies, Blood and Wolfe made no effort to conceptualize recreational behavior of families as a familial role.

Komarovsky (1962) also presents a rather descriptive view of leisure activities among the working class although she does indicate that recreational choices and decisions are likely to be a function of the more general normative context of the family. She states:

> The differences in the extent of joint social life appear to be explained less by external obstacles than by attitudes towards it. Neither presence or absence of young children, length of residence in the community, or level of income affects the relative frequency of joint social contacts [1962: 317].

Connor et al. (1955) found a relationship between recreation and one aspect of role behavior. They found that fathers who viewed their role as traditional were more likely to participate in recreation with their children than fathers who viewed the role of a good father as developmental.

Both Komarovsky and Connor et al. suggest that recreational activity might be related to other family expectations, but neither goes further to conceptualize a recreation role. Gerson (1960: 360) pretty well sums up the family recreation research by stating:

> Empirical studies of leisure behavior have tended to emphasize the allocation of available time to various types of activity with the relative neglect of dynamic variables related to satisfactions from leisure or to motivations behind the choice of leisure time activities.

Perhaps the closest to a role formulation is found in Ogburn (1938) in his inclusion of recreation as a family function and in Bates (1956) in his inclusion of "playmate" as a role in the position of mother and father. However, neither pursues the delineation in detail nor develops indicators for measurement.

Thus, there is considerable evidence that recreation is highly valued and some clues that spouses feel some sense of duty with respect to it, but specific conceptualization is lacking in the literature and research to test the existence of the norm and supporting sanctions is missing. Therefore, we treat the role as hypothetical—believing that it exists but feeling that documentation is needed before it can be taken for granted.

NORMATIVE ROLE DEFINITION

Our conceptualization of role utilizes the existence of norms as the primary indication of role existence. The existence of norms is measured here by two questions. One question asks which spouse (if either) should organize and carry out family recreation; a second question asks whether respondents disapprove of a spouse who fails to organize and carry out family recreation. The latter is considered a sanction to enforce the norm.

The degree to which spouses perceive societal norms existing in the realm of recreation will both affect and reflect the importance attached to family recreation. Increased time and financial re-

sources for recreation in the family is a relatively recent phenomenon. As a result, one would expect the normative aspects of
such a role to be somewhat vague compared to the more traditional family activities which would likely be prescribed to certain
family members and have strong sanctions attached to enforce
them. Numerous research studies, for example, show strong prescriptions attached to housekeeping, child care, and provider roles.
Conversely, one would expect that family activities which have
recently emerged as a result of societal change would be less
subject to strong role expectations. Family recreational behavior
would be such an area. Thus, one would expect a wider variation
in the responsibilities for providing family recreation, if, in fact,
such responsibilities are felt to exist.

As can be seen from Table 8.1, the greatest proportion of both
spouses indicated that the responsibility to provide for family
recreation is optional as long as it is done. More husbands than
wives indicated that the role behavior should be joint, whereas
more wives felt it was no one's duty. In other words, more
husbands attached normative expectations to family recreation
than wives. The fact that a large proportion of both spouses
indicated that the responsibility should be optional as long as it is
done indicates that there are minimum expectations as to *who* will
perform the role. Yet the feeling that it should be done gives
support to the hypothesized existence of such a *parental* role.

Another measure of the strength of the norms associated with a
given role is the strength of the negative sanctions applied for
failure to carry out the role. An indication of such sanctions is
measured here by the disapproval toward a spouse who fails to
organize and carry out family recreation. Thirty percent of the
wives would strongly disapprove and another forty-two percent
less strongly. The respective proportion for husbands was thirty-
four and fifty-four percent (Table 8.2).

The previous finding that fewer wives endorse the normative
dimensions of the role than husbands is further reinforced here.
Over twice as many wives (twenty-eight compared to twelve percent of husbands) indicate that it makes no difference if a spouse
refuses to organize and carry out family recreation.

In sum, most respondents feel that there are family recreational

Table 8.1.

NORMATIVE PRESCRIPTIONS AND ENACTMENT OF THE RECREATIONAL ROLE: BY REPORT OF HUSBAND AND WIFE

NORM: Whose duty is it to organize and start family recreation?

Who Should Organize	HUSBANDS' REPORT		WIVES' REPORT	
	N	%	N	%
Husband entirely	4	1.9	2	1.0
Husband more than wife	31	15.0	12	5.9
Husband and wife both the same	81	39.3	66	32.5
Optional—it doesn't matter as long as it is done	83	40.3	108	53.2
Wife more often than husband	3	1.5	3	1.5
Wife entirely	1	0.5	..	0.0
It is no one's duty	3	1.5	12	5.9
TOTAL	206	100.0	203	100.0

ENACTMENT: Who is it who usually organizes it and gets it started?

Spouse Who Organizes	HUSBANDS' REPORT		WIVES' REPORT	
	N	%	N	%
Husband always	6	3.0	5	2.5
Husband more than wife	71	35.5	57	28.2
Husband and wife both the same	65	32.5	70	34.7
Wife more than husband	53	26.5	56	27.7
Wife always	5	2.5	6	3.0
Other	..	0.0	6	3.0
No one	..	0.0	2	1.0
TOTAL	200	100.0	202	100.1

Table 8.2.
COMPETENCE AND STRAIN IN THE RECREATIONAL ROLE: AS REPORTED BY HUSBANDS AND WIVES

COMPETENCE: How well do each of you do in organizing and starting family recreation?

HOW WELL DO YOU DO?	PERCEPTION OF THE HUSBAND BY HIMSELF		PERCEPTION OF THE HUSBAND BY WIFE		PERCEPTION OF THE WIFE BY HERSELF		PERCEPTION OF THE WIFE BY HUSBAND	
	N	%	N	%	N	%	N	%
Extremely well	12	6.1	14	7.0	6	3.0	14	7.0
Very well	42	21.2	49	24.4	33	16.3	58	29.1
Fairly well	97	49.0	90	44.8	112	55.4	99	49.7
Not very well	39	19.7	33	16.4	45	22.3	23	11.6
Not at all well	8	4.0	9	4.5	6	3.0	4	2.0
Not done	...		6	3.0	...		1	0.5
TOTAL	198	100.0	201	100.1	202	100.0	199	99.9

STRAIN: How do you feel about your participation in recreation with your family?

FEELING ABOUT PERFORMANCE	HUSBANDS' REPORT		WIVES' REPORT	
	H	%	H	%
I worry frequently	40	19.4	37	18.0
I worry once in a while	48	23.3	40	19.4
I don't think much about it	30	14.6	32	15.5
I usually feel good about it	64	31.1	82	39.8
I am completely satisfied	24	11.7	15	7.3
TOTAL	206	100.1	206	100.0

responsibilities, but they do not assign them to a particular spouse. Rather, they indicate that they should be optional as long as they were done or that both spouses should have equal responsibility. While some type of sanctions are applied by most, more express mild disapproval, suggesting that normative prescriptions may be less fully developed and strongly held in this as compared to some other roles. It might be suggested that this role would be more parental than specifically that of a father or mother role; parents are more likely to feel responsibilities toward providing recreation for their children than for each other. Also, husbands seem to hold stronger role prescriptions than wives. This may reflect the husbands' absence from the family. Thus, they may have stronger feelings about family recreation than wives, who are with children more.

ENACTMENT OF THE RECREATIONAL ROLE

Normative prescriptions provide guidelines for role behavior. The more fully crystalized these prescriptions, the more likely that behavior will be consistent with the norms. This assumes that costs will be greater for those who deviate from strong normative expectations than from weak ones. In that a recreational role seems to exist in some families in varying degrees and in some not at all, one would also expect a wider variety of behavior than would be the case in roles with more fully crystalized expectations.

Role enactment seems to follow prescriptions with the exception that husbands feel they carried out more of the responsibilities whereas more wives indicate a joint responsibility (Table 8.1).

A comparison of expectations and enactments indicate some discrepancy between norms and behavior. A considerable number of both husbands and wives indicate that the responsibilities should be optional or joint whereas both spouses indicate that behavior is more husband-oriented. This might be viewed as a potential source of conflict in some families; more so by husbands in that they perceive a stronger normative definition of the role for themselves. In other families, it may only involve an allocation of duties to the spouse with more time available.

EVALUATION OF ROLE PERFORMANCE

This section of the analysis focuses on attitudes toward the importance of family recreation to the spouses, the competence of spouses in enacting the role, and the amount of time spent in recreational activities.

ROLE COMPETENCE

Role competence was measured by asking respondents how well they do in organizing and providing recreation for their family. In addition, respondents were asked to indicate how well their spouses carried out the role.

The largest percentage of both husbands and wives believe that they do only fairly well at providing for family recreation (Table 8.2). Only about one-fourth of the respondents indicate that they do very or extremely well in carrying out the role. Both husbands and wives perceive their spouses as more competent than the spouses view themselves. Husbands perceive wives as substantially more competent than wives perceive themselves, whereas wives perceive husbands as only slightly more competent than husbands perceive themselves. The explanation of why many spouses seem to do only fairly well in carrying out this role is not obvious. Perhaps it is related to the newness of this type of role in our society; families may have few standards upon which to base their evaluation. Also, it may be that it is difficult to find recreation attractive to both sexes and several ages of children and parents.

TIME FOR FAMILY RECREATION

Another indicator of family members' evaluation of their role behavior was their feeling about the amount of time spent in family recreation. In our study, respondents were asked whether or not they were satisfied with the amount of time they spent in family recreation. Over three-fourths of both spouses indicated a desire for more family recreation, and none preferred less than they had currently. Husbands tended to indicate a greater desire for much more family recreation than did wives. Perhaps this was a function of the husband being away from home more than the wife.

Value on the Recreational Role: Spouses were asked how important it was for them to have family recreation together. Each respondent was also asked to indicate his or her perception of the spouse's feelings as to the importance of family recreation.

Approximately three-fourths of both spouses viewed family recreation as quite or extremely important to them. Husbands tended to perceive family recreation as slightly more important to wives than the wives reported. On the other hand, wives perceived family recreation as less important to husbands than the husbands reported.

Such findings suggest that perhaps there is some confusion between spouses as to the importance of family recreation, but they reaffirm the greater importance to husbands than to wives. These findings are not entirely in accord with Blood and Wolfe's (1960), which emphasize the importance to wives of couple recreation. However, the above data are for family as contrasted to couple recreation.

Role Strain: Respondents were asked how much they worried about the way they carried out the recreational role. Table 8.2 shows forty-three percent of the husbands and thirty-seven percent of the wives felt some worry about their role performance. While a substantial proportion of both spouses seems concerned about their role performance, husbands are more likely than wives to worry. This is likely to be a function of the provider role being primarily associated with husbands, thus removing them from the family. Also, more husbands agree that they have a duty to provide recreation for their families. In other words, more husbands hold strong norms about providing family recreation. Thus, the potential for guilt would be more likely to exist.

DISAGREEMENTS IN FAMILY RECREATION

Conflict in the recreational role was measured by asking spouses how often they argued about family recreation.

About one-fourth of our couples report conflict "frequently" or "sometimes" (Table 8.3). This places it fairly high in conflict

Table 8.3.

CONFLICT AND ITS RESOLUTION IN THE RECREATIONAL ROLE: ives BY REPORT OF HUSBANDS AND WIVES

CONFLICT: How frequently, if ever, do you and your wife openly disagree or argue concerning recreation?

FREQUENCY OF DISAGREEMENT	HUSBANDS' REPORT		WIVES' REPORT	
	N	%	N	%
Very frequently	2	1.0	1	0.5
Frequently	3	1.5	2	1.0
Sometimes	41	20.0	48	23.6
Seldom	102	49.8	96	47.3
Never	57	27.8	56	27.6
TOTAL	205	100.1	203	100.0

RESOLUTION OF CONFLICT: If there is a disagreement concerning recreation, who makes the final decision?

SPOUSE WHO MAKES DECISIONS	HUSBANDS' REPORT		WIVES' REPORT	
	H	%	N	%
Husband always	11	5.6	14	6.9
Husband more than wife	51	25.9	69	33.8
Husband and wife the same	75	38.1	54	26.5
Wife more often than husband	27	13.7	18	8.8
Wife always	: :	0.0	: :	0.0
Absolutely no disagreements	33	16.8	49	24.0
TOTAL	197	100.1	204	100.0

among familial roles. Only child socialization clearly is a more conflicted role, with kinship at about the same level (see Table 9.8). Recreational conflict is slightly less prominent, at least comparatively, in ours than in the Blood and Wolfe research (1960). However, they were dealing more specifically with husband-wife than with family recreation, so the data are not entirely comparable. There is some reason to believe, too, that difficulties in enacting the child socialization role may have increased considerably, and with it, conflict in that role since 1960.

POWER IN THE RECREATIONAL ROLE

Respondents were asked who made the final decision if spouses were unable to agree. Some disagreement concerning disagreement was disclosed. Twenty-four percent of the wives but only seventeen percent of the husbands denied any disagreement over recreation (Table 8.3). Of those reporting disagreements, more husbands reported equality in resolving the issues. However, more of the wives said that husbands got their way more often. Few of either sex report the patriarchal pattern of issues as always resolved in favor of the husband. It is apparent, therefore, that unshared power is a rare phenomenon, but whether it is shared equally or with more to the husband depends on whether it is the perception of husbands or wives.

SUBCULTURAL AND SITUATIONAL VARIATION

One would predict that recreational role expectations would be affected by a number of subcultural variables. This is based on the notion that role expectations are likely to be a function of the value orientations of the spouses. Yet, in a given family, the behavior related to these basic expectations is likely to be modified by various situations unique to a family. For example, a husband may *enact* part of the housekeeper role if the wife is employed even though it is opposed to his basic role expectations (norm); if he does not do it, it likely will not get done.

EMPLOYMENT OF THE WIFE

For the wives' responses, the socioeconomic variables related to their own employment and educational status were important. Wives in white-collar occupations were more likely to have husbands who carried out recreational duties. This may be a result of pressure on the time available to the wife in that the findings also indicated that wives who were employed long hours were more likely to have husbands who enacted the recreational role. Thus, the time factor might be an important criterion for role enactment, at least from the wife's perspective; when she worked, the husband was more likely to enact the role. In addition, the length of her work week was important. Wives employed forty hours were more likely to feel that they were fairly or very competent than was any other group. Those employed more than forty-eight hours were least likely to feel they enacted the role well. The feeling of personal competence has been reported as positively related to maternal employment by several authors (e.g., Hoffman and Nye, 1974). However, employment more than forty hours may result in too little time available to devote to the recreational role.

Desired amount of participation in family recreation as reported by wives is affected only by the wife's work status. The longer the work week of the wife, the greater the proportion who desire much more family recreation. It seems that spouses who are away from their homes seem to desire more family recreation than those who are home. Perhaps family recreation is used to compensate for feelings of guilt that may be associated with spending time away from home. Conversely, people who are at home a lot might like to get away from it and do things alone.

For wives' responses, the length of the wives' work week reduced the error of prediction most. Those who worked more than forty hours per week more frequently felt guilt, followed closely by those who worked forty-hour weeks. Those who were not employed outside the home and those who were employed less than forty hours per week were least likely to express guilt.

Other Social Variation: A number of socioeconomic and religious differences were found, but most were not theoretically meaningful and might have only reflected accidental sampling differences. One possible explanation for the paucity of meaningful subcultural differences is that two response categories in the normative question might tap the same universe of beliefs; that is, (1) the response category that husband and wife have equal responsibility for the role, and (2) it doesn't matter which does it, provide it is done.

Conceptually, they differ because the first anchors the role in *both* positions, while the second commits it only to one or the other spousal position. Still, the distinction may not have been clear to all respondents.

However, some interesting differences did emerge. Catholic and Fundamentalist Protestant couples were more likely to prescribe the role for husbands, which is congruent with other ideological beliefs concerning the husband as head of the family. Role enactment, however, did not follow this ideology. In families with preschool children (ages two to five), the wife was more likely to enact the recreational role, while the husband was more likely to do so in families with no preschoolers. This is consistent with studies showing that, during the period with preschool children (provided there are less than four children), the wife tends to take more responsibilities other than the provider role (Campbell, 1970). With no preschool children, she is more likely to share the provider role and her husband to share more of the other roles.

IMPLICATIONS

Almost all respondents see the providing or expediting of recreation for family as the duty of spouses and parents; however, a majority of women and a large minority of men see it only as the duty of one or the other adult family member, which might as well be done entirely by one or the other or divided equally or in any other way. Another substantial minority see it as a responsibility to be shared equally. Therefore, perhaps the best statement that can be made is that, normatively, it is a shared role. Sanctions are present to enforce it. Yet, these are relatively mild sanctions compared to those for some of the more traditional family roles (see Table 9.1).

In terms of our original hypothesis that a recreational role is emerging, the data support the hypothesis. However, the emergence of this role has likely not proceeded to its fullest development. Yet it might be that the norms and expectations in this area of family functioning will continue to remain somewhat flexible. As a result, we suggest that more research focus on this area of family life, especially in light of the rapid changes occurring in the recreational climate of the American society. An important aspect of future research should center on the definitions that may be attached to both family and individual recreational activities. Also, the effects of recreational activities on other family activities and on general family interaction should be investigated. There is some tendency of ministers and others dealing with family problems to prescribe more family recreation as a treatment for family conflict or the alienation of family members from each other. We would question such prescriptions, yet more research will be required to develop answers to this and related questions.

Chapter 9

FAMILY ROLES IN COMPARATIVE PERSPECTIVE

F. Ivan Nye

Each role has been analyzed with respect to a set of role properties ranging from normative prescriptions to role conflict and its resolution (Chapters 3-8). It is the purpose of this chapter to compare these properties among roles. For example, where are the norms most prescriptive, where most permissive, where is the most role strain, the most role conflict, and so forth?

NORMS AND SANCTIONS: SHARING AND SEGREGATION

In recent years, a trend has developed toward sharing role enactment, with more women taking paid employment and more men helping with child care and housekeeping. We have noted, too, the development of a new cast to the male sexual role. The question to be explored here is to what extent the sharing of role enactment has entered into the culture of American society to modify the traditional normative structure of familial roles.

PROVIDER AND HOUSEKEEPER ROLES

Our data suggest that rather major changes have occurred. In the provider role, traditionally limited to the male domain, over

half the women now feel that it ought to be a shared responsibility, although with somewhat more responsibility retained by
men. Almost forty percent of the husbands agree. It is still a long
way to complete sharing of this role, but the size of the change to
date seems impressive.

The housekeeper role has been the natural paired role with
provider. In traditional thinking, the husband brought home the
bacon and the wife cooked it. Again, the data suggest major
changes, even greater than those in the provider role from such
norms of segregation. Over *half of both sexes* indicate that housekeeping is a shared responsibility, although more of it still belongs
to the wife (Table 9.1).

The validation of the norms regarding family roles involves the
application of sanctions. Duty without enforcement tends to be
meaningless. It will be recalled that respondents were asked
whether, if a person willfully failed to enact a role, the respondent
would disapprove and/or would ostracize him or her by not
choosing him or her as a friend, not socializing with him or her,
not permitting children of the families to play together, or pref-
erring he or she not live in the same community. The data suggest
that much greater consensus exists with respect to the provider
than with respect to the housekeeper role. Over eighty percent
would ostracize non-role enactment in the provider role, but fewer
(nearly half) would do so in the housekeeper role. Ninety-five
percent of both sexes would strongly disapprove nonperformance
of the provider role by men (Table 9.2). We think the present data
provide evidence of the normative decline of the housekeeper role.
The self-deprecatory admission that "I'm only a housewife" seems
to be currently rooted in the feeling that these tasks are not very
vital to the welfare of family members. Perhaps this is due to the
ready availability of canned food, cooked bakery products, TV
dinners, and the availability of restaurants, laundries, and other
facilities which can effectively handle many housekeeping tasks.

A large proportion of husbands share this role, but fewer do so
than either sex feels should be the case. Put another way, most
men (seventy percent) say they should share housekeeping tasks,
and more (fifty-six percent) say they *do* share them than wives
report. Only fifty-four percent of the women see the husband as

Table 9.1.
NORMATIVE CONTENT OF FAMILY ROLES BY SEX OF RESPONDENT (in percentages)

ROLE	Husband Solely	Husband Mainly	Equal	Wife Mainly	Wife Solely	No One, Other or Optional	Total
SOCIALIZATION OF GIRLS							
Wives' Reports	0	1	56	43	1	0	101
Husbands' Reports	0	1	53	46	0	0	100
SOCIALIZATION OF BOYS							
Wives' Reports	0	32	61	7	0	0	100
Husbands' Reports	2	32	60	7	0	0	101
CHILD CARE							
Wives' Reports	0	3	44	51	1	0	99
Husbands' Reports	1	7	63	28	0	0	99
PROVIDER							
Wives' Reports	37	55	3	4	0	0	99
Husbands' Reports	57	38	3	2	0	0	100
HOUSEKEEPER							
Wives' Reports	0	0	1	54	42	2	99
Husbands' Reports	0	0	1	70	25	3	99
THERAPEUTIC							
Wives' Reports*							
Husbands' Reports*							
SEX (available)							
Wives' Reports	1	**	87	1	**	11	100
Husbands' Reports	1	**	91	1	**	7	100
KINSHIP (own kin)							
Wives' Reports	0	1	11	41	29	17	99
Husbands' Reports	3	9	14	38	14	21	99
RECREATIONAL							
Wives' Reports	1	6	33	2	0	59	101
Husbands' Reports	2	15	39	2	1	42	101

* The role cannot be divided, but sixty-one percent of the women affirmed that women have a duty to enact the role. Sixty-nine percent of the men took a similar position with respect to men's duties (see Figure 7.1).

**Question was not asked in this form.

Table 9.2.

SANCTIONS FOR NONCOMPLIANCE WITH THE NORMS
OF FAMILY ROLES BY SEX OF RESPONDENT (in percentages)

ROLE	OSTRACISM	STRONG DISAPPROVAL	WEAK DISAPPROVAL	NO OSTRACISM	NO DISAPPROVAL
SOCIALIZATION					
Wives' Reports	81	*	*	19	*
Husbands' Reports	81	*	*	19	*
CHILD CARE					
Wives' Reports	86	*	*	14	*
Husbands' Reports	83	*	*	17	*
PROVIDER					
Wives' Reports	81	95	3	19	2
Husbands' Reports	84	95	2	16	3
HOUSEKEEPER					
Wives' Reports	62	*	*	38	*
Husbands' Reports	45	*	*	55	*
THERAPEUTIC					
Wives' Reports	*	64	23	*	13
Husbands' Reports	*	70	24	*	7
SEXUAL					
Wives' Reports	*	67	17	*	16
Husbands' Reports	*	81	9	*	10
KINSHIP					
Wives' Reports	*	45	42	*	13
Husbands' Reports	*	33	42	*	25
RECREATIONAL					
Wives' Reports	*	30	42	*	28
Husbands' Reports	*	34	54	*	12

*Question not asked for that role.

having housekeeper duties, and fewer (thirty-nine percent) agree that their husbands actually do share the role. These data suggest several conclusions: (1) men are ahead of women in accepting the norm of shared responsibilities in the housekeeper role. Almost three-fourths in our sample accept it; (2) enactment of the role by men lags considerably behind the normative position both as reported by men and women; and (3) women less than men perceive participation by men in the role. Putting these together, men are more ready attitudinally to share this role, and more of them (than women) perceive themselves as participating in it.

A different situation holds with regard to the provider role. More women than men see a duty for women to share in the provider role (fifty-five versus thirty-eight percent). The proportion who actually do so, in terms of taking paid employment, falls about midway between the normative position of men and women. Taken together, data from the two traditionally sex-segregated roles suggest that, as norms and behavior move toward role-sharing, each sex is more ready to assume responsibilities in the role of the other than are the members of that sex ready to re-evaluate the role in terms of sharing responsibility between spouses.

CHILD CARE AND SOCIALIZATION ROLES

Child care has been thought of as primarily a duty of mothers rather than of fathers, while child socialization has been shared, with the sex of the child influencing the amount of responsibility allotted to each parent.

Undoubtedly, the age of the child affects both the norms of child care and the enactment of the role. Preschool children are viewed as more nearly falling entirely within the responsibility of the mother, since a majority of them spend daytime hours in the care of their mothers. With enrollment in school, the child's hours in the home more nearly correspond with those of the father. Also, a majority of mothers who take paid employment do so when there no longer are preschool children at home.

With such traditional notions in mind, it is a little surprising that most of these parents felt that both parents have *equal* responsibility for both roles, with the minor exception that a little fewer than half the mothers view child care as an equally shared role. Large minorities see child socialization as sex-linked, with fathers primarily responsible for boys, mothers for girls. However, even these respondents place role enactment as shared rather than segregated. *Less than five percent* of our respondents view either child care or socialization as the sole responsibility of one or the other sex. Sanctions to enforce these roles are, like those associated with the provider role, endorsed by the vast majority of parents.

The enactment of these roles is far different from the norms. The mother dominates the socialization of girls and the child care role. Even in the socialization of boys, a larger proportion is done by mothers than by fathers. These roles, then, are characterized by equalitarian norms in terms of duty of mothers and fathers but, in practice, mothers carry out more of the responsibilities of the two roles. Yet, it would be inaccurate to think of either of these roles as rigidly segregated. It is the unusual family in which one parent takes total responsibility (Table 9.3).

KINSHIP AND RECREATION ROLES

Our previous analyses suggest that these two roles share some common characteristics, but not necessarily for the same reasons. Both are normatively defined, but less strongly reinforced by sanctions than the others. In addition, both are seen by an appreciable proportion of respondents as optional—it matters not which spouse enacts them.

Each respondent was asked whose duty it was (if anyone's) to keep contact with kin by writing or phoning. Duties in this role are heavily weighted toward the wife. With reference to her relatives, only one percent of the wives feel it is primarily the duty of the husband and only eleven percent feel that the husband has an equal duty. In contrast, five percent of the husbands feel that keeping in touch with the husband's relatives is the duty of the wife and only twelve percent view it as primarily their own responsibility. Of all the roles in this study, the kinship role as we

Table 9.3.

ENACTMENT OF FAMILIAL ROLES* AS REPORTED BY WIVES AND THEIR HUSBANDS (in percentages)

ROLE	HUSBAND SOLELY	HUSBAND MAINLY	EQUAL	WIFE MAINLY	WIFE SOLELY	NO ONE, OTHER OR OPTIONAL	TOTAL
SOCIALIZATION OF GIRLS							
Wives' Reports	0	1	25	71	3	0	100
Husbands' Reports	0	3	28	66	3	0	100
SOCIALIZATION OF BOYS							
Wives' Reports	2	21	33	45	0	0	101
Husbands' Reports	1	25	38	33	2	0	99
CHILD CARE							
Wives' Reports	2	2	19	73	3	1	100
Husbands' Reports	2	8	29	58	3	0	100
PROVIDER							
Husbands' Reports	57	36	4	2	0	0	99
HOUSEKEEPER							
Wives' Reports	0	0	1	47	50	1	99
Husbands' Reports	0	1	1	56	39	2	99
KINSHIP (yours)							
Wives' Reports	1	2	11	54	30	1	99
Husbands' Reports	10	25	16	40	6	3	100
RECREATIONAL							
Wives' Reports	3	29	35	28	3	3	101
Husbands' Reports	3	36	32	27	3	0	101

*It is not possible to think of allocation of sexual duties between spouses, since it must occur in interaction. However, the question was asked, "When you desire sex and your spouse does not, how does she (he) respond?" Only eight percent of wives said the husband usually does not respond, but twenty-nine percent of the husbands reported that the wife usually did not respond.

Since each enacts the therapeutic role for the other, it is not possible to think of it in terms of enactment by one sex or the other. However, each was asked how the spouse usually responded when a problem was shared with them. Seventy percent of the husbands usually made a positive attempt to help, compared with eighty-five percent of the wives. Twenty percent of husbands responded by listening passively, compared to ten percent of the wives. Seventeen percent of the husbands and ten percent of the wives tried to avoid sharing the problem or made a negative response to the spouse (Figure 7.1).

have presently analyzed it is most heavily normatively weighted toward one sex—the female. However, almost one in five sees it as the duty specifically of neither husband nor wife. About half of these see it as a duty which one or the other should perform, but of no consequence which, while the remainder feel there are *no* duties to keep in communication with kin.

The normative content of the recreational role is still more diverse. While a substantial minority view it as equally the duty of husband and wife, a majority of women (fifty-three percent) and a plurality of men (forty percent) indicate that it is optional—i.e., someone should organize and promote recreation for family members, but it does not matter whether it is the husband or the wife who assumes the responsibility. Logically one could add these to the number who say it is equally the responsibility of husband and wife, resulting in a proportion of over eighty percent who see these duties as not especially centered in either the mother or father position! It is not that there are no recreational duties—only two percent of husbands and six percent of wives said that—but overwhelmingly in this role it is seen as someone's duty, not especially one or the other parent's.

Sanctions to enforce these roles are comparatively weak. A minority of either sex would feel strong disapproval of a spouse who failed to enact either of these roles. Women are a bit more concerned about the kinship role; men, about the recreational. If milder forms of disapproval are also taken as being or implying sanctions, then a large majority support the norm, but still support is weaker than for the other six roles. We think that both roles are viewed as less crucial than other family roles. However, recreation, not previously conceptualized as a duty, appears to be increasing in importance. If that direction continues, it may rank with older, established roles in importance. In contrast, the kinship role is well established traditionally but apparently has been undermined by increased geographic mobility, public and private insurance for such contingencies as old age, loss of employment, loss of the provider by death, crippling illness, and the like. Despite the fact that kin continue to play a part in recreational and emotional life, apparently communication with kin is no longer viewed by the adults in our sample as a strong obligation.

THERAPEUTIC AND SEXUAL ROLES

It is hardly possible to contrast shared with segregated roles insofar as sexual and therapeutic duties are concerned, since therapeutic involves services of one spouse to the other and sexual behavior involves both in any interaction. We did ask husbands and wives whether each sex had a duty to be available when the other desired intercourse (Table 9.1). About ninety percent (slightly more men than women) replied in the affirmative. A slightly higher proportion of women rejected any idea of duty in sexual intercourse.

About sixty percent of women and seventy percent of men affirm a duty for their sex to enact the therapeutic role. This clearly refutes the idea in earlier family literature that this is exclusively a duty of women. Despite the recency of the conceptualization of the therapeutic and sexual role for men, both are recognized as duties by sizable majorities in this sample.

Sanctions supporting these roles are much stronger than for the kinship and recreational roles, but much less than for the provider role. Appreciable numbers would not disapprove of role refusal by either sex. This level of sanction supports the hypothesis of the existence of both roles, but indicates a lesser intensity of support for their enforcement, *and* a minority of spouses dispute the normative content of the sexual and therapeutic roles.

Regarding the sexual role, husbands appear more willing to fulfill their marital obligations than are wives. Only eight percent of the wives reported that the husband usually is unresponsive to their sexual interest. In contrast, twenty-nine percent of husbands stated that wives usually did not respond to their sexual interest. Thus, general agreement exists that each spouse has a duty to meet the sexual needs of the other and both would strongly disapprove a clear failure to interact sexually, but a much larger proportion of wives are unwilling to participate. The fact should not be disregarded, however, that in participating in intercourse many husbands fail or only succeed partially in meeting their wives' sexual needs.

If sexual role enactment is more often inadequate by women, therapeutic enactment is more often refused or only passively enacted by men. In both roles, considerable disparity exists between the normative prescriptions of the roles and role enactment—especially of wives in the sexual and husbands in the therapeutic role.

ROLE ENACTMENT

All of the family roles include a normative structure enforced by sanctions. In general, role enactment corresponds to the normative structure, but the fit between norms and behaviors is far from perfect.

A strong tendency toward equality in family roles is shown in the normative structure of the family, this being the modal response for the child care, child socialization, sexual, and recreational roles. In a sense, this is true of the therapeutic role, since a sizable majority feel that each sex should enact it for the other. Enactment, however, varies considerably from these norms. Mothers dominate the child care role and the socialization of girls. Even the socialization of boys, where men might be expected to be more active, tips toward role enactment by mothers (Table 9.3). Men take more initiative and are more responsive in the sexual role. Only in the recreational role do the norm and role enactment agree on equality. Provider and housekeeper roles, normatively defined as shared unequally, show role enactment which corresponds roughly to norms although men share the housekeeper role less frequently than either sex thinks appropriate. The kinship role tends to be viewed as a female role, and role enactment generally corresponds to the norm. Finally except for the sexual role, where a disparity exists between norm and behavior, a larger proportion of women enact the roles than either sex agree that they should. We shall return to this disparity in our consideration of role conflict.

EVALUATION OF ROLES

LeMasters has said of the enactment of parental roles that it bears a resemblance to service in the armed forces—in that some volunteer, while others are drafted (LeMasters, 1974). He goes on to observe that family roles are hard, complicated work which, at the same time, provide many rewards. In this section, we shall see how spouses evaluate their own and their spouses' role performance, how many of them find more rewards than costs in these roles, and which roles they value more than others.

ROLE COMPETENCE

Most respondents feel they do well in their parental and provider roles. Especially, a large majority of mothers and fathers feel well satisfied with their enactment of the child care role. Perhaps it is because the role is viewed as important, yet the criteria for good performance are fairly clear-cut and within the capabilities of most parents. A larger proportion have some reservations about their performance of the socialization role (Table 9.4). Here, the appropriate goals and the means of control and motivation of children are more often in doubt. The school, peer group, and sometimes the two parents embrace different goals or different strategies in inculcating norms and values, and in controlling behavior.

Wives provide a generally positive evaluation of their spouses' competence in the provider role, but many men do not concur. The self-evaluation in this instance seems more accurate than that of the spouse. The most favorable response category was worded "exceptionally competent." Only ten percent of the husbands make this claim, while forty percent of the wives evaluate their husbands in such generous terms. This apparent inflation by the wife of the husband's competence is limited to this one role. In most of the roles, the wife's evaluation of her husband is lower than his evaluation of her and little different from his evaluation of his own role performance. Whether this apparent inflation in the provider role represents her real perception, or whether in this especially crucial male role wives intentionally inflate the husbands' performances, cannot be determined from the present data. Taking his evaluation of his role competence, we find that many men have major reservations about their competence in this role. It is one which they can only partially control, since it depends on the number and types of jobs available in a society which chroni-

Table 9.4.

ROLE COMPETENCE OF SELF AND SPOUSE BY SEX OF RESPONDENT
(in percentages)

Role	Very Good	Good	Fair	Poor or Don't Enact	Total
CHILD SOCIALIZATION					
Wife, self-report	7	67	23	2	99
Wife, husband's report	15	62	20	4	101
Husband, self-report	11	62	22	5	100
Husband, wife's report	14	61	21	4	100
CHILD CARE					
Wife, self-report	30	66	4	0	100
Wife, husband's report	30	62	8	0	100
Husband, self-report	24	61	14	2	101
Husband, wife's report	29	58	8	4	99
PROVIDER					
Husband, self-report	10	44	41	4	99
Husband, wife's report	40	35	21	4	100
HOUSEKEEPER					
Wife, self-report	6	34	52	8	100
Husband, self-report	6	22	36	36	100
THERAPEUTIC					
Wife, self-report	8	39	42	12	101
Wife, husband's report	23	50	20	7	100
Husband, self-report	13	46	30	12	101
Husband, wife's report	16	38	30	17	101
KINSHIP					
Couple—wife's report	3	28	60	10	101
Couple—husband's report	1	28	51	20	100
RECREATIONAL					
Wife, self-report	3	16	55	25	99
Wife, husband's report	7	29	50	15	101
Husband, self-report	6	21	48	25	100
Husband, wife's report	7	24	45	24	100

cally has more workers than positions. We did not in this study ask wives to evaluate their own provider role.

Of the other roles, respondents rate themselves and their spouses next highest in the therapeutic role. Husbands and wives generally agree quite closely on the evaluation of the husband's competence. Actually, the wives rate their husbands a little lower than the husbands rank themselves. A much larger discrepancy exists between the self and spouse ranking of the wife. Only eight percent of wives rate themselves as doing extremely well in the role and forty-seven percent as above the fair category. Almost three times as many husbands give their wives top rating and almost three-fourths rate their wives above fair. In this instance, the husbands' perceptions appear more accurate. Eighty-five percent of the wives enact the role positively and actively compared to seventy percent of the husbands (see Chapter 7). While all who provide positive, active response to the husbands' problems may not be effective in helping solve them, it does appear that more wives are effective than are husbands, simply because more try. It is not clear why some wives apparently underestimate themselves in this role; perhaps because their lack of technical information concerning their husbands' job problems may lead them to underestimate the value of their therapeutic response.

Neither men nor women are very optimistic about their performance of the housekeeper, kinship, or recreation roles. Only thirty to forty percent rate themselves or their spouses above the "fair" category. The housekeeper and kinship are long-established traditional roles, but there is much evidence of their decline. Other agencies can and do provide alternatives to these roles which family members have so long performed. We would venture a bit further and suggest that many tasks are *better* performed by alternative agencies. Clothing manufacture, canning, and baking come to mind. Perhaps these are not better in an absolute sense, but they allow women to use their time more profitably. The care of the sick by the medical profession and the support of the orphans and aged persons by Social Security are examples of alternatives to the kinship role.

We find it difficult to advance a single hypothesis for the low level of role competence in the recreational role. It is a new one in the normative sense. It could be that effective strategies for role enactment have not been sufficiently developed or tested. It may be an especially difficult role because of the wide range of interests and capabilities among family members. Or it could be that it still has a low priority, as we have inferred is true of the housekeeper and kinship roles.

Looking at the seven roles (no report of competence was requested on the sexual role), respondents evaluate themselves and their spouses highest on the child care role, but very high on socialization, too. Next, in a mid-position, are the provider and therapeutic roles—one traditional, one emerging. Finally, most feel only modestly competent at best in housekeeper, kinship, and recreation roles.

IDENTIFICATION WITH ROLES

Some roles become so rewarding that the role player is unwilling to relinquish them even if the prescribed duties could be legitimately performed by someone else. That is, rewards are built into the interaction involved in the role, so that one does not wish to relinquish it. Apparently this is true for some people with respect to the parental roles. Also, this seems to be true of some occupational roles. On the other hand, some may be ambivalent concerning a role while still others may dislike it vehemently.

Our strategy for obtaining a person's attitude toward a role was to ask, "Suppose you had a very large income for life, making it possible to hire a well-trained person to help with the above tasks. Do you think you would do so?" This was asked for the child care, socialization, and housekeeper roles. Roughly equivalent questions were also formulated for the provider and therapeutic roles. The question did not seem appropriate and was not asked for the sexual role, the kinship, or the recreational role.

If we have succeeded in tapping identification with roles, then a majority of both men and women do not wish to delegate more of the child socialization or child care roles to other people, although some ten to fifteen percent would like to do so (Table 9.5). It is important here to remember that about one-third of preschool children are currently being cared for by someone other than the mother while she is at work. The addition of fifteen percent to this would bring the figure to nearly one-half. Fewer fathers than mothers indicate a desire for a decrease from their current involvement in the role. Of course, their present involvement is, in most families already less and they are able to participate on a more selective basis. If one adds the "might" category to those who would relinquish all or part of the role, then the proportion is nearer one-third for mothers and one-fifth for fathers who would like to decrease or terminate their enactment of these parental roles.

Women show no such reticence with respect to the housekeeper

Table 9.5.

IDENTIFICATION WITH ROLES BY SEX OF RESPONDENT
(in percentages)

WOULD LIKE SUBSTITUTE FOR ROLE

ROLE	Certainly Would	Probably Would	Might	Probably Would Not	Certainly Would Not	Total
CHILD SOCIALIZATION						
Wives' Reports	3	10	22	34	32	101
Husbands' Reports	3	6	13	42	35	99
CHILD CARE						
Wives' Reports	2	10	22	41	25	100
Husbands' Reports	3	5	14	49	29	100
HOUSEKEEPER						
Wives' Reports	21	28	24	18	8	99
Husbands' Reports	9	17	27	34	13	100

PROVIDER: If you were wealthy would you continue to work for pay?

	Would Retire	Other Responses	Change Jobs	Stay With Same Job	Total
Husbands' Reports	22	7	29	42	100

THERAPEUTIC: Do you want to help (husband, wife) with (his, her) problems?

	Other Responses	Almost Always	Always	Total
Wives' Reports	1	43	56	100
Husbands' Reports	2	54	44	100

role. Almost half would or probably would be glad to reduce or eliminate their roles as housekeeper. If those who respond "might want to do so" are included, the proportion is almost three-fourths.

Most men seem to have some identification with the provider role, since about seven in ten would work at some kind of productive labor, but about a quarter of the younger middle-aged men *would give up the provider role entirely*. Probably some of those who would change jobs would do so in order to work only part of the year, shorter hours, or some other reduction in their provider role, although present data do not indicate how large this proportion would be.

Our data on the therapeutic role seem inadequate, since we asked how they felt about helping the spouse. What is needed is data on how many would prefer that the spouse consult a professional counselor, provided one were readily available. Without such an alternative, almost all indicate they "almost always" wish to assist with the problems of their spouse.

VALUE PLACED ON THE ROLE

The value one places on a role and one's identification with it seem interrelated, but are not identical. A mother can highly value good child care, for example, without wanting to provide it herself on a twenty-four-hour-a-day basis.

Comparing Tables 9.5 and 9.6, one sees similarities in the identification with, and the value placed on, the child socialization and child care roles. Competent role enactment in both is very highly valued, and only a minority of parents are ready to further share or delegate these responsibilities. The housekeeper role provides an interesting contrast. A majority of women are ready to delegate part or all of it, but a large majority highly value a well-kept home. They like the end product, but they have little identification with cooking, cleaning, laundering, and mending. Men agree in placing a relatively high value on competent housekeeping. Since men are only marginally involved in housekeeping, we are not sure how to evaluate their lesser interest in reducing or eliminating their participation in the role. If the data mean what they seem to, then many men are not averse to doing some household tasks. We would like to see more investigation of this idea before accepting it, however.

Respondents were asked how important having a high income was to them. Undoubtedly, the answers would have been different if the question had been how important it was to have a steady income which would cover the basic needs of their families. Given that the question focuses on high income, not too many respondents value this extremely highly. Even so, about fifty percent report "highly" or "extremely highly," which is about the same as the valuation placed on competent role enactment in the kinship role.

The relatively low value placed on the therapeutic role is probably also at least partially due to the wording of the item. Respondents were asked, "How important is it to you to have

Table 9.6.
VALUES ON ROLES BY SEX OF RESPONDENT (in percentages)
IMPORTANCE OF THE ROLE

Role	Extreme	High	Some	Little or None	Total
CHILD SOCIALIZATION					
Wives' Reports	78	22	0	0	100
Husbands' Reports	74	26		0	100
CHILD CARE					
Wives' Reports	79	21	0	0	100
Husbands' Reports	71	27	1	1	100
PROVIDER					
Wives' Reports	9	33	47	12	101
Husbands' Reports	12	41	39	7	99
HOUSEKEEPER					
Wives' Reports	19	55	23	3	100
Husbands' Reports	21	53	25	1	100
KINSHIP					
Wives' Reports	15	46	30	10	101
Husbands' Reports	6	43	36	15	100
THERAPEUTIC					
Wives' Reports	20	26	23	31	100
Husbands' Reports	16	21	20	44	101
SEXUAL					
Wives' Reports	24	49	22	5	100
Husbands' Reports	37	48	13	2	100
RECREATIONAL					
Wives' Reports	29	49	20	3	101
Husbands' Reports	27	54	16	3	100

someone with whom to share your problems?" Having someone to talk with does not necessarily mean one will get competent assistance in solving the problem. Presumably, if getting *effective* help with problems had been included in the statement, the value indicated for the therapeutic role would have been greater.

Sex is highly valued, somewhat more by men than by women. Family recreation is also valued by most of the respondents of both sexes. Respondents were asked how important sex is in their marriage, and how important it is to them that their family have recreation together.

Differences in wording of the questions limit the comparability of the values placed on the eight roles. Therefore, the comparison above and in Table 9.6 should be considered preliminary. However, in the hierarchy of family values, it appears that good care and training of children comes first. Moderately high values seem present for a well-cared-for home, family recreation, and sexual intercourse. Competent performance of the kinship role ranks considerably lower. We would anticipate that a more adequate measure of the provider role would indicate a high value on it, but additional data are needed here as well as in measuring the value of the therapeutic role.

STRESSES IN ROLE ENACTMENT

We have selected three aspects of role stress for analysis in this study: (1) one's feelings of adequacy or inadequacy in role enactment, (2) the amount of role conflict one experiences with one's spouse, and (3) in whose favor the conflict is resolved. Perceived inadequacy comes sometimes from comparing one's performance with some standard of what one should do or should not do. It may also stem from what one thinks that reference groups expect of one occupying a certain position or constellation of positions.. If performance exceeds these, one presumably feels satisfied with role enactment; if it falls short, one feels anxious.

Role conflict is seen as stemming from inadequate role performance as viewed by the spouse or what Kirkpatrick (1963) and Turner (1970) call role dissensus. Turner sees role dissensus as occurring when members are using different criteria in the judgment of adequacy (Turner, 1970). For example, the father who disciplines a child employing corporal punishment may feel he is enacting the child socialization role competently while his wife, rejecting that strategy, may disagree completely. A third major source of role conflict arises from conflicting demands of roles either in the same position or in different positions (Goode, 1960). Thus, mothers may experience conflict between their provider and child care roles.

ROLE STRAIN

If worrying about one's role performance is a useful indicator of role strain, then our sample of parents-spouses gives considerable evidence of role strain (Table 9.7). About half of both men and women report worrying about their performance of the child socialization, therapeutic, and recreational roles, as well as a like proportion of women in the housekeeper and men in the provider roles. In contrast, only about one-fourth of men and women worry about the child care role, as do about the same proportion of men with regard to their kinship and sexual roles. More women (about one-third) report strain in the latter two roles. At the other end of the attitudinal continuum, the highest proportion of men and women are satisfied with their performance in the child care and sexual roles. Relatively few of the respondents lacked a definite feeling about their role enactment—positive or negative—especially in child care, child socialization, provider and house-keeper roles. In the roles which are normatively less clearly defined, a more substantial number simply have given little thought to their role enactment. Three of these—sexual (male), recreational, and therapeutic—we have characterized as emerging roles with duties not yet felt by some. Kinship seems to be moving the other way, toward an exit from the normative structure (Table 9.7).

The child socialization and child care roles provide an interesting contrast. Both are valued about equally highly, but more parents feel sure of their competence in child care and fewer worry about role performance. Apparently the complexity of child socialization, variation in goals between parents and extra-familial agencies, and the difficulty in achieving desired socialization goals, leads to appreciable anxiety for about half the parents in our sample.

We are a little surprised at the proportion of women worrying about their housekeeper role. Many show little identification with the role and report they do not perform it well. It would seem that this low performance together with a relatively high value on a well-kept home leads to anxiety. In general, the same combination of low ratings of self-competence together with a moderately high value on the recreational role may explain the large proportion who worry about their performance in the recreational role.

The large proportion reporting worry about the therapeutic role cannot be explained the same way, since fewer indicate a high

Table 9.7.

ROLE STRAIN BY SEX OF THE RESPONDENT (in percentages)

FEELINGS ABOUT ROLE ENACTMENT

Role	Frequent Worry	Occasional Worry	No Reaction	Generally Satisfied	Completely Satisfied	Total
SOCIALIZATION						
Wives' Reports	26	30	1	38	4	99
Husbands' Reports	17	31	4	41	7	100
CHILD CARE						
Wives' Reports	8	16	1	60	15	100
Husbands' Reports	11	15	4	51	19	100
PROVIDER						
Husbands' Reports	25	20	5	41	10	101
HOUSEKEEPER						
Wives' Reports	19	29	8	37	7	100
KINSHIP						
Wives' Reports	13	21	21	37	8	100
Husbands' Reports	5	20	32	29	13	99
THERAPEUTIC						
Wives' Reports	21	27	11	36	5	100
Husbands' Reports	21	27	11	33	8	100
SEXUAL						
Wives' Reports	11	25	8	38	19	101
Husbands' Reports	8	15	11	42	24	100
RECREATIONAL						
Wives' Reports	18	19	16	40	7	100
Husbands' Reports	19	23	15	31	12	100

value on the role. However, we have suggested earlier that the item measuring the value of the therapeutic role is probably inadequate. The prevalence of worry about one's performance in this role gives added credence to that suggestion. There is an air of consistency about the kinship role. The normative content is low, it is valued relatively low, many report lack of competence in role enactment, and few worry about their performance in it.

The normative content of the provider role is especially high and a large minority of men rank themselves modestly in role competence. The role does not rank high by our measure of value, but it may be recalled that that item measured value on a high income rather than an adequate income and therefore we think it gives an unrealistically low estimate of the value of that role. The prevalence of anxiety in performance of this role supports this interpretation.

If we were to rank the eight roles in terms of role strain, child socialization would clearly head the list. Following it would be a group of roles about equally characterized by strain, including the provider, housekeeper, therapeutic, and recreational. Finally, relatively low in role strain, we find the sexual, kinship, and child care roles. Some, but relatively few, are concerned about their performance in these roles.

ROLE CONFLICT

The measure of conflict developed in this study is one of overt conflict and does not include disagreement which is not verbalized. The distribution of nonverbal conflict might be somewhat different, as might its resolution.

Reports of very frequent or frequent conflict over any of the familial roles is low—so low it seemed parsimonious to combine the categories. It is not surprising that the largest proportion reporting conflict is in the child socialization arena (Table 9.8). Perhaps more illuminating is the small proportion reporting no conflict in that role—only about ten percent compared to double, triple, or even larger proportions in the other roles. Provider and housekeeper roles seem least characterized by conflict, perhaps because they are the most segregated in terms of responsibility (Table 9.1). Ninety-nine percent of the respondents agreed the housekeeper role was solely or mainly the responsibility of the wife, and about ninety-five percent agreed that the provider was wholly or mainly the responsibility of the husband. Also, these facts deal more with objects or with people outside the family group, whereas the other roles focus on aspects of family interaction.

Frequent conflict in the other roles—child care, kinship, and recreational—is reported by only a few couples. These roles are intermediate between child socialization as a high conflict role and the provider and housekeeper roles which are low.

Previous research which directly addresses the issue shows that wives more frequently exercise a veto on intercourse by virtue of the fact that more of them desire it infrequently (Chapter 6). Spouses who do not wish to have intercourse are more likely to refuse than to accede to the spouses' interests (Burgess and Wallin, 1953). Husbands have many more sexual complaints than do

Table 9.8.

CONFLICT IN ROLES BY SEX OF RESPONDENT (in percentages)

Role	Very Frequent or Frequent	Sometimes	Seldom	Never	Total
SOCIALIZATION					
Wives' Reports	7	37	47	9	100
Husbands' Reports	6	34	48	11	99
CHILD CARE					
Wives' Reports	0	15	51	33	99
Husbands' Reports	4	20	54	22	100
PROVIDER					
(Husband's Occupation)					
Wives' Reports	1	10	32	58	101
Husbands' Reports	5	10	38	47	100
PROVIDER					
(Wife's Occupation)					
Wives' Reports	1	12	20	67	100
Husbands' Reports	4	7	29	60	100
HOUSEKEEPER					
Wives' Reports	2	16	41	40	99
Husbands' Reports	3	20	45	31	99
KINSHIP					
Wives' Reports	5	18	51	26	100
Husbands' Reports	3	21	50	26	100
RECREATIONAL					
Wives' Reports	1	24	47	28	100
Husbands' Reports	2	20	50	28	100

wives. We do not know how many of these kinds of dissatisfactions reach the open conflict stage—probably not very many, since most couples do not communicate freely about sexual interests, needs and behavior. Probably most conflict in this role is nonverbal and expressed convertly, if at all.

In the child care, provider (both husband and wife's jobs) and housekeeper roles, considerably more wives than their husbands reported "no conflict." We have no very good post hoc hypothesis to offer as an explanation of this. It *may be* relevant that wives are more likely to verbalize their dissatisfactions than are husbands. In a study of divorce complaints, it was found that wives verbalized about double the number of dissatisfactions compared to husbands (Levinger, 1966). It is also possible that more husbands experience conflict but do not express it. They see conflict in the situation, but the wife does not because the husband does not verbalize his position. The weakness in this argument, is that the question asked for "open conflict." If it were indeed open, the wives would have been aware of it and presumably would have reported it—as did their husbands.

RESOLUTION OF ROLE CONFLICT

It would seem that responsibility, role enactment, and authority should be closely correlated. In principle, they would be identical. If so, then the spouse with primary responsibility would enact most of the role most of the time and, if differences developed concerning the role, such differences would be resolved in his or her favor. Again, when viewing the data on conflict resolution, one should remember that it is open conflict rather than total disagreement to which the data refer.

More decisions go to the husband than to the wife in the child socialization, provider (his occupation), recreation, and kinship (his kin) areas. More go to the wife in the housekeeper, child care, provider (her occupation), and kinship (her kin) realms. Large numbers of couples report an even number of decisions going to husband and wife in the child socialization, child care, kinship and recreational roles.

While the above resolution of conflict seems to correspond in general with normative and role enactment characteristics of the role, the correspondence is not very close. Thus, in the child care role, about half feel that mother and father have equal responsibility for the role and about half feel that it is primarily the mother's responsibility. In the enactment of the role, two-thirds of the mothers more frequently enact the role, yet in resolving conflict only about half the decisions favor the wife. In the socialization role, parents are viewed as having similar duties, but mothers enact more of the role, and yet more of the open disputes are resolved in favor of the husband. In the housekeeper role, ninety-nine percent see it as more the duty of the wife, and in ninety-nine percent of families, mothers do more of the housekeeping, yet in about one family in six either more of the disputes are resolved in favor of the husband, or resolved equally between spouses. Thus, while there is a general correspondence between norm, behavior, and authority, in an appreciable number of families wives have less authority than the norms or their role enactment would predict. To determine the amount of discrepancy existing between norm, enactment, and authority, a rough score was devised as follows: If the norm gave equal responsibility to husband and wife, score 0; if more to wife, score wife +1, husband −1; if sole responsibility to wife, score wife +2, husband −2. The husband's score becomes the reciprocal of that of the wife.

In Table 9.10, we see that the norms accord more responsibility to the wife in the socialization of girls, child care, housekeeper, and kinship roles. In the last, even responsibility for keeping contacts with the husband's relatives is more often accorded to the wife. Enactment generally follows the norms with one major exception. The socialization of boys is seen as more the responsibility of fathers than mothers, but both sexes agree that mothers actually enact the role more than do fathers.

The division of power is considerably at variance with both responsibility and role enactment. Men have more responsibility in about two and one-half roles: socialization of boys, provider, and recreational roles. In only one, the provider, do they clearly enact more of the role, yet they exercise more or equal power in disputed decisions in all roles except the housekeeper. This contrast seems especially strange in the socialization of girls and in the child care roles in which the norms accord the mother the responsibility. She typically discharges more of the responsibilities but wins no more than half of the openly disputed issues. This holds also for the kinship role.

It is possible that the wife wins more decisions in which the husband disagrees but allows the decision to go her way without dispute. As noted above, Levinger found that husbands are less likely to protest elements of their wives' behavior of which they disapprove than are wives to protest their husbands' actions (Levinger, 1966). Unless this is true, there is a major disparity between role norms and power to make decisions which could be a major source of discontent of wives in marriage.

Table 9.9.
RESOLUTION OF CONFLICT BY SEX OF RESPONDENT (in percentages)

Role	Husband Always	Husband More	Equal	Wife More	Wife Always	No Conflict	Total
SOCIALIZATION							
Wives' Reports	12	38	27	17	0	6	100
Husbands' Reports	9	35	30	18	2	6	100
CHILD CARE							
Wives' Reports	6	15	24	26	1	27	99
Husbands' Reports	5	24	31	24	3	12	99
PROVIDER (Husband's Occupation)							
Wives' Reports	36	16	4	1	0	43	100
Husbands' Reports	36	23	8	1	1	31	100
PROVIDER (Wife's Occupation)							
Wives' Reports	9	8	8	14	9	52	100
Husbands' Reports	6	8	10	22	13	42	101
HOUSEKEEPER							
Wives' Reports	2	4	7	45	7	34	99
Husbands' Reports	1	8	8	45	15	22	99
KINSHIP (Your Kin)							
Wives' Reports	5	8	43	14	2	28	100
Husbands' Reports	8	31	36	5	1	20	101
RECREATION							
Wives' Reports	7	34	27	9	0	24	101
Husbands' Reports	6	26	38	14	0	17	101

Conflict Resolved in Favor of

Table 9.10.

COMPARISON OF THE NORM, ROLE ENACTMENT AND AUTHORITY IN DISPUTED DECISIONS BY SEX OF RESPONDENT

	Normative Score	Enactment Score	Authority Score
SOCIALIZATION OF GIRLS			
Wives' Reports	+ .4	+ .5	- .6*
Husbands' Reports	+ .6	+ .7	- .5*
SOCIALIZATION OF BOYS			
Wives' Reports	- .2	+ .3	- .6*
Husbands' Reports	- .3	+ .1	- .5*
CHILD CARE			
Wives' Reports	+ .5	+ .4	0.0
Husbands' Reports	+ .1	+ .5	- .1
PROVIDER			
Wives' Reports	-1.3	-1.6	-1.5
Husbands' Reports	-1.5	-1.6	-1.4
HOUSEKEEPER			
Wives' Reports	+1.3	+1.4	+ .7
Husbands' Reports	+1.1	+1.2	+ .8
KINSHIP (own kin)			
Wives' Reports	+1.2	+1.1	0.0
Husbands' Reports	+ .4	0.0	- .5
RECREATION			
Wives' Reports	- .1	0.0	- .5
Husbands' Reports	- .3	- .1	- .3

*Only one score was obtained for the resolution of disputes with respect to socialization; that is, separate scores were not obtained by the sex of the child. Positive scores indicate more duty, enactment, or authority by wives; negative scores, more by husbands.

PART III

FAMILY ROLES AS SOCIAL EXCHANGE

ROLE ANALYSIS AND SOCIAL EXCHANGE

The role concept is independent of any one theoretical system. In fact, it is employed in most theoretical approaches and conceptual frameworks for the study of the family. One of these is the set of theoretical propositions about social behavior which is, in sociology, usually identified under the umbrella of "social exchange." This tag is not entirely satisfactory because some of its more seminal concepts have come from reinforcement theory, which does not necessarily utilize the idea of exchange (Simpson, 1972). Nonetheless, social exchange is the most widely used label for this general set of ideas, and will be used here with the qualification that some of the key concepts employed are from the related but not identical heritage of reinforcement theory.

Some of the basic ideas in social exchange theories have a long history in the sociology of the family, being readily traced to Willard Waller (1937). However, they have lain dormant until general theories of social exchange were elaborated by Thibaut and Kelley (1959), Homans (1961), Blau (1964), and recently updated by Simpson (1972), Homans (1974), and Ekeh (1974).

In the early 1960s, roughly equivalent concepts were being employed without being identified as social exchange concepts: for example, Blood and Wolfe's resource theory of family power (1960) and Farber's theory of permanent availability (1964). More recently, Richer (1968) and Edwards (1969) have drawn attention to the potential of this system of concepts and propositions for interpreting family structure and interaction. This potential has experienced some additional development since then; for example, Bartz and Nye utilized it to analyze causes and consequences of early marriage (1970); Goode (1971) employed it in his discussion of violence in the family; Scanzoni (1972) interpreted changes in sex roles; Arnott (1972) analyzed the decision of married women whether or not to take employment; and Edwards (1973) utilized it to analyze parent-youth conflict.

In these final two chapters, family roles are utilized as the carriers of rewards from one spouse to the other and of rewards from parents to children. While it implies, and to some small extent measures, rewards which are returned by the receiving spouse, it is not necessary to think of the reciprocating immediately. Burns (1973) has shown that in what he terms "friendship" categories, one may reward a friend without an immediate return of the favor. The "relationship is rewarding," which we interpret to mean that the friend will from time to time return a reward to his friend in various ways. Thus, the relationship is profitable to both even though it does not involve an immediate reward returned to the "sender." Ekeh (1974) shows that this is also true of mutual help groups, who keep a mental account of the rewards they have received. It may be a period of weeks or months before they reciprocate with appropriate help. In case of serious illness or major injuries, there may be no expectation that the services will be repaid, unless the rewarder should experience a disability himself.

In Chapter 10, Bahr proposes that the more competent a spouse is in enacting roles (the more he or she rewards the spouse), the more power the spouse allows him or her in that role. In Chapter 11, Nye and McLaughlin hypothesize that the more a spouse rewards the other spouse, the more profitable the relationship and the better satisfied the second spouse is with the marriage.

Chapter 10

ROLE COMPETENCE, ROLE NORMS,
AND MARITAL CONTROL

Stephen J. Bahr

The sources of marital control have been a frequent topic of research and discussion. Perhaps the best-known attempt to explain marital control is Blood and Wolfe's (1960) resource theory. Despite considerable research on this topic, adequate tests of their theory have not been conducted (Safilios-Rothschild, 1970). This paper attempts to deal with some of the conceptual ambiguities and methodological problems of earlier studies. The resource theory will be reformulated using family role and social exchange concepts, and then subjected to an empirical test.

RESOURCE THEORY

Blood and Wolfe (1960) hypothesized that the comparative competence of husband and wife is the primary source of marital control. Thus, "Caspar is henpecked because he is incompetent and makes very little contribution to the life-satisfactions of his wife" (Blood and Wolfe, 1960: 13). This has become known as the "resource theory." Blood and Wolfe say (1960: 12):

The sources of power in so intimate a relationship as marriage must be sought in the comparative resources which the husband and wife bring to the marriage, rather than in brute force. A resource may be defined as anything that one partner may make available to the other, helping the latter satisfy his needs or attain his goals. The balance of power will be on the side of that partner who contributes the greater resources to the marriage.

The only requirement of a resource is that it be relevant to the needs of one's spouse. It could be anything including physical attractiveness, prestige, housekeeping skills, or the ability to earn money. A resource need not have objective reality, although it must be perceived as such. A husband's control over a wife depends on his resources compared to hers. If either her needs or his ability to provide decrease, his control over her will decrease (Wolfe, 1959).

The dependent variable in this theory is control or power. Power is the term usually employed in the literature. In this paper, the term control is preferred because it appears more precise in its connotations than power. Control is defined as the degree to which one partner complies with the other in the face of conflict. It is a continuous variable ranging from complete husband control to complete wife control. The situation where one controls as frequently as the other is the middle point of the continuum and is termed equalitarian.

The resource theory is congruent with the notion of social exchange. The central thesis of social exchange theory is that people attempt to maximize their profits by maximizing rewards and minimizing costs. It follows from resource theory that the more rewards (satisfaction of needs) one receives from one's spouse, the more likely one is to comply with the spouse when differences of opinion arise. In a sense, such an exchange is balanced in that resources are traded for compliance. In another sense, this type of exchange is not balanced in that the one with fewer resources must give in. Even so, it is assumed from exchange theory that obtaining the resources and giving compliance is more profitable than noncompliance in the absence of the resources.

It should not be inferred from this discussion that one partner always gives in to the other. In one situation the husband may give in while at another time the wife may defer. Sometimes compliance might appear too costly and the exchange may not take place. The result may be unresolved conflicts and a withholding of resources. It should also be emphasized that control in one area does not necessarily imply control in another area. There may or may not be a relationship between control in one area and control in another.

FAMILY ROLES

The relationship between resources and control will be examined using the concept of family role. A discussion of the role concept and delineation of eight family roles was presented earlier in this volume. The child socialization, child care, provider, housekeeper, and recreation roles provide data appropriate for the purposes of this study.

There are a number of reasons why family roles were used to analyze resources and control. First, since these roles have been the focus of other theorizing and research, the study will be integrated into a meaningful set of concepts. Second, some of the problems of using resources or control as global concepts will be eliminated since a meaningful set of dimensions is provided by the various roles. This allays one of the frequent criticisms of studies of marital power.

Should global assessments be desired this can be obtained by combining the five roles. Five roles is a small enough number that control is not divided into an unmanageable set of categories. Third, this categorization of marital control is not completely arbitrary since it is based on five family roles, each with a set of tasks, norms, and sanctions.

ROLE COMPETENCE

One of the primary resources in marriage appears to be competent performance of family roles. In fact, Blood and Wolfe (1960) used the terms resources and competence interchangeably. Inade-

quate performance would be a cost, while competent role enactment would be rewarding. For example, a wife obtains monetary
and social rewards if her husband has a high-paying, prestigious
job. In most families, adequate performance of child socialization,
child care, housekeeping, provider, and recreation tasks is valued
and contributes to goal attainment. It follows that rewards will
increase as competence in role performance increases. These ideas
can be summarized in the following propositions:

(1) The more competent one's role performance, the greater the rewards
    to one's spouse.

(2) The greater the rewards provided to one's spouse, the more likely the
    spouse will comply in the face of conflict.

(3) The more competent one's role performance, the more likely the
    spouse will comply in the face of conflict.

NORMS AND CONTROL

Norms specify some roles as the husband's domain and others as
the wife's. Departure from these expectations could produce role
strain which reduces the profit from an exchange. Thus, compliance with norms regarding control would be profitable and would
therefore influence the actual control structure of marriage. For
example, the norms may state that the husband should have the
final say in the provider role. If the husband is also the more
competent, the reward-cost outcome would be increased, thereby
increasing the husband's control. However, if the wife is the more
competent but the spouses feel the role should be the responsibility of the husband, the effects of these two factors operate in
different directions. The rewards from the wife's competence
would be offset by costs of norm violation. Similarly, an equalitarian norm would tend to produce an equalitarian control structure. The strain resulting from norm violation would increase costs
which offset the rewards of competence.

Norms regarding role competence may also affect costs. For
example, if it is not considered proper for a wife to earn more
than her husband, the rewards from her earning power may be

neutralized by the costs of this norm violation. The value of role performance would be expected to affect reward-cost outcomes in a similar way. The more important a role, the more rewarding competence in that role would be. Therefore, it is expected that the relationship between competence and control would be greater for highly valued roles. However, one complicating factor is that compliance might be more costly for highly valued roles.

HYPOTHESES

Since the concept resource is similar to that of reward, the resource theory may be restated as follows: The greater the rewards one provides for one's spouse (relative to the rewards one receives from the spouse), the greater one's control over the spouse. However, according to exchange theory, goodness of outcomes depend upon rewards and costs, not simply rewards. Therefore, an implicit assumption of the resource theory is that costs are held constant. Perhaps one of the reasons that tests of the resource theory have not been conclusive is that costs have been ignored. Resources would not be expected to be correlated with control if they also had a positive relationship with costs.

From the proposition that control depends upon rewards and costs, the following hypotheses have been derived:

(1) The more the role competence of one spouse exceeds that of the other, the more likely (with respect to that role) that the marital control of that spouse will exceed that of the other.

(2) If the norms assign responsibility for making role decisions to one spouse, then it is more likely that disputed decisions will be resolved in favor of that spouse.

The third hypothesis is a combination of hypotheses one and two:

(3) The greater the association between relative husband-wife competence and norms about control, the greater the association between relative competence and marital control.

This hypothesis is a restatement of the reward-cost principle. It states that ability to predict control will be greatest when competence and norms operate in the same direction. For example, the husband's control is expected to be greatest when he is more competent than the wife and when the norms prescribe him as the one who should have control.

The final hypothesis is:

(4) The more important a role, the greater the association between relative competence and marital control.

This hypothesis assumes that the more important a role, the more rewarding competence will be. It also assumes that, as importance increases, the rewards of compliance are greater than the costs. In this paper, tests of hypotheses 1 through 3 are reported. These hypotheses are tested within each of the five family roles discussed earlier. Hypothesis 4 cannot be adequately tested with the present data.

MEASUREMENTS

To measure control, each couple was asked who makes the final decision if there is disagreement. For example, for the child socialization role, the question was as follows: "If there is disagreement concerning the teaching and disciplining of your children, who makes the final decision?" The responses to each question were (1) husband always, (2) husband more than wife, (3) husband and wife exactly the same, (4) wife more than husband, (5) wife always, and (6) absolutely no disagreement.[1]

Competence was assessed by asking each partner how effective he or she and spouse were at performing the tasks for each of the five roles. For example, in the child socialization role the question was as follows: "All things considered, how effective do you think each of you are [sic] at teaching your child the things he or she needs to know in order to be able to take care of himself and get along with others?" The responses were (1) extremely effective,

(2) quite effective, (3) somewhat effective, (4) not very effective, and (5) not at all effective.

Blood and Wolfe emphasized that tests of the resource theory require an assessment of relative husband-wife competence—i.e., of which spouse has the greater competence. To do this, we computed the difference between the husband's and wife's competence in each role, and have called this *relative competence*. Throughout the analysis, the discussion of competence refers to relative competence, except for the provider role, where only the husband's competence was assessed.

Norms of control were measured by asking each respondent who should have the right to make the final decision in each of the five roles. Responses were (1) husband always, (2) husband more than wife, (3) husband and wife exactly the same, (4) wife more than husband, and (5) wife always.

FINDINGS

The data relevant to hypotheses 1 and 2 are presented in Table 10.1. Hypothesis 1, that the more competent spouse is more likely to win disputed decisions, is supported in the child socialization, child care, and recreation roles. In each role, relative competence has a significant association with control as reported by both husbands and wives. The correlations are somewhat stronger in the wives' than in the husbands' data. In the provider and housekeeper roles, hypothesis 1 is not supported.

Hypothesis 2 states that, in a role in which the norms assign responsibility for role decisions to one spouse, it is more likely that disputed decisions will be resolved in his or her favor. The data are consistent with this hypothesis in all roles except the housekeeper role. In that role, the husbands' data support the hypothesis while the wives' do not. In the other four roles, the correlations of the husbands and wives are of similar magnitude. It would appear that norms, *as measured here,* have a greater influence on control than relative competence.

The third hypothesis is an attempt to take rewards and costs

Table 10.1.

RANK ORDER CORRELATIONS OF MARITAL CONTROL
WITH RELATIVE COMPETENCE AND NORMS OF
CONTROL, BY FAMILY ROLES AND SEX

Family Role	Independent Variable	Kendall's Tau-b Husbands	Wives	Partial Tau-b[a] Husbands	Wives
Child Socialization	Relative Competence	.11*	.24*	.09	.22
	Norms of Control	.23*	.20*	.22	.18
Child Care	Relative Competence	.17*	.19*	.14	.19
	Norms of Control	.15*	.17*	.11	.17
Provider	Relative Competence	.003	.01	-.01	.004
	Norms of Control	.12*	.17*	.12	.17
Housekeeper	Relative Competence	.05	.09	.03	.09
	Norms of Control	.16*	.05	.16	.04
Recreation	Relative Competence	.12*	.19*	.10	.16
	Norms of Control	.23*	.25*	.22	.23

N = 211

*Statistically significant

[a] This is the correlation between control and each independent variable while controlling for the other independent variable. This is what Smith (1972) refers to as an ordinal path coefficient and was computed using the following formula:
$$T_{yx.z} = (T_{yx} - T_{yz} T_{xz}) / (1 - T_{xz}^2).$$

into account simultaneously. The two basic questions are: (1) Is competence correlated with control when the norms of control are held constant? (2) How well can control be predicted from both competence and norms? The first question can be answered by computing partial correlation coefficients. These are presented in Table 10.1 and are very similar to the bivariate coefficients. The data provide evidence that the effects of competence on marital control are independent of the effects of norms on marital control.

To answer the second question in hypothesis 3 requires an examination of control within the different combinations of competence and norms. For example, we would expect equalitarian marital control when norms are equalitarian and the husband's competence the same as the wife's. Unfortunately the sample is too small to adequately examine all the different combinations of norms of control and relative competence. The data are therefore only suggestive regarding this aspect of the analysis.

In the child socialization role, the effects of norms and competence appear to operate as hypothesized. The percentage of equalitarian families is greatest when the norms are equalitarian and the competence of husband and wife equal. The control of husbands is greatest when the husband is the more competent and the norms are patriarchal. The data for the child care role are similar. Husband control appears greatest when the perceived norms and competence both favor the husband, while the percentage of families in which the wife has greater control than her husband is highest when the norms are matriarchal and she is the more competent spouse. However, when child care norms are equalitarian, the data are less conclusive. In this situation competence is related to control in the wives' data while this relationship is not evident in the husbands' responses.

A particularly interesting interaction between norms of control and competence occurs in the provider role. Although competence has no direct effect on control, it influences the relationship between norms and control. When husbands are perceived to be exceptional providers, there is a moderate relationship between norms of which spouse should control and actual marital control. This association declines when husbands are viewed as being better than average but not exceptional providers. When husbands are perceived to be average or below average providers, the association between norms and control is negligible. These data are presented in Table 10.2. It appears that patriarchal norms may cease to be an

Table 10.2.

RANK ORDER CORRELATIONS BETWEEN MARITAL CONTROL AND NORMS OF CONTROL FOR THE PROVIDER ROLE, BY HUSBAND'S COMPETENCE AS A PROVIDER

Husband's Competence as a Provider	Kendall's Tau-b			
	Husbands	N	Wives	N
Exceptional Provider	.33*	20	.23*	78
Better than Average Provider	.16*	90	.14*	69
Average or Below Average Provider	.05	81	.07	43

*Statistically Significant

important source of control for husbands *if they are not competent providers.* There was no relationship between competency and marital control in the housekeeper role and adding the normative prescription of control does not change this.

In the recreation role, the findings are similar to those in the child socialization and child care roles. The control of the husband tends to be strongest when the norms are patriarchal and he is more competent than the wife. The proportion of couples that have an equalitarian control structure in the recreation role is greatest when the norms are equalitarian and husband and wife are equally competent.

As mentioned above, an adequate test of hypothesis 4 is not possible with these data. This is primarily because little variation exists in role importance in the socialization, child care, and housekeeping roles. In addition, a measure of the importance of the provider role is not available.

IMPLICATIONS

Both comparative role competence and role norms need to be included in a social exchange approach to marital control. Both affect it independently and they interact, at least in the provider role, so that incompetence in the role neutralizes the effect of the norm which assigns decisions in it to the husband.

Incorrect inferences are likely to result if either competence or norms are ignored. However, even the combination leaves much of the variance in marital control unexplained. Some, perhaps much, of this could be explained by a more complete conceptualization and measurement of the ability of the spouse to inflict costs on the marital partner.

The use of social exchange theory appears to have clarified the way resources and norms may affect control. It seems that some of the confusion regarding the resource theory has existed because cost factors have not been taken into account along with the reward factors, which must be done to provide an adequate test of theories of marital control.

NOTE

1. These responses seem to be irrelevant to the analysis. First, they were included as equalitarian relationships, then the analyses were recomputed excluding them. Their inclusion or exclusion had no effect on the analysis. The percentage of respondents who stated that they had absolutely no disagreement with respect to each role was as follows: child socialization—six percent; child care—twenty percent; provider—thirty-five percent; housekeeper—twenty-seven percent; recreation—nineteen percent.

Chapter 11

ROLE COMPETENCE AND
MARITAL SATISFACTION

F. Ivan Nye and
Steven McLaughlin

Attempts to predict marital satisfaction largely preoccupied family sociologists for two decades following the publication of Burgess and Cottrell's *Predicting Success or Failure in Marriage* (1939). While scholars were able to "explain" statistically a major amount of variance in the dependent variable—marital satisfaction, marital adjustment, or a closely related concept—little progress was made in *why* certain experiences, attitudes, or characteristics of individuals were related to successful and/or permanent marriages.

It is not our purpose here to review in detail or to summarize the voluminous research which followed the Burgess-Cottrell and later Burgess-Wallin (1953) studies. A relatively comprehensive review has been made by Hicks and Platt (1970) and a listing of propositions by Goode et al. (1971) and Burr (1973).

As noted in the introduction to Part III, the recent use of social exchange can be dated from Waller's Rating and Dating Hypothesis (1937). Sporadic use of some of the ideas, especially those involving rewards, are found from 1960 to 1968. Since the latter date, an increasing number of family sociologists have employed some exchange concepts as theory. One of these, Nye et al. (1973) derived a number of propositions relating social exchange concepts to marital satisfaction.

THE PROBLEM

If family roles encompass the essential activities of family life, then it follows that the more competently one spouse enacts these roles, the more rewards he or she provides for the other spouse. If these rewards are at least at one's comparison level (what one feels a spouse should provide), then he or she should be satisfied with the marriage, provided costs are not excessive. The role competence of one spouse may increase the goodness of outcomes of the other in another way; that is, many family roles are shared and a good performance by one's spouse lightens one's own tasks, thereby decreasing costs. Since satisfaction is a variable, it would appear that the more rewards the spouse provides, the better satisfied one would be with the marriage. The problem presently addressed, then, is to test the proposition that the degree of role competence in one's several family roles is related to the spouse's satisfaction (dissatisfaction) with the marriage. If there is indeed a relationship, what part of marital satisfactions and dissatisfactions can it explain?

PROFITS, STABILITY, AND MARITAL SATISFACTION

The central idea in social exchange theories is that individuals select their activities and interaction in ways that maximize (or are expected to maximize) their profits (or goodness of outcomes). Therefore, it follows that if a spouse enacts his (her) roles competently, supplying high rewards without exacting high costs from the spouse, then the spouse is likely to be satisfied with the outcomes of the relationship. That spouses who are competent in performance of family-relevant roles provide high rewards to their respective spouses is clear, but that such role enactors provide higher profits or better outcomes does not *necessarily* follow (although we hypothesize that they do). It might be that competent people require a higher level of role performance from other group members, which may increase the costs of other group members or they may expect more autonomy for themselves or grant less of it to other group members, thereby increasing the costs of the other members of the group. Still, it seems probable that increases in cost (if any) are likely to be less than the greater rewards derived from superior role enactment. Based on this reasoning, a number of propositions are derived from exchange theory, some of which can be tested with present data:

(1) Persons who enact their group roles competently provide greater rewards for others than those whose role enactment is less competent.

(2) Individuals who supply more rewards to other group members are more likely to provide better reward-cost outcomes for them.

(3) Individuals who are perceived as providing good reward-cost outcomes to group members are likely to be liked and valued by other group members.

(4) Individuals who are perceived as providing better reward-cost outcomes to other group members are more likely to receive good reward-cost outcomes in return.

(5) Individuals (and couples) who receive good reward-cost outcomes from each other are likely to be satisfied with their marriages.

(6) Individuals (and couples) satisfied with their marriages are less likely to dissolve them through divorce or separation.

Proposition 1 presumably is true. In fact, it appears almost tautological. Two is plausible, but has not to our knowledge been tested. We shall not be able to test it directly, but an indirect test will be provided by testing the relationship of role competence to marital satisfaction. If greater role competence results in better reward-cost outcomes, then an increase in rewards exceeds the increase in costs. Proposition 3 is central to the exposition of social exchange ideas by both Thibaut and Kelley (1959) and Homans (1961). It will receive an indirect test by the same means as 2.

Propositions 4, 5, and 6 have had less attention previously, and merit discussion. Since we like those who provide good reward-cost outcomes for us, we reward such individuals partly by liking them and showing appreciation and gratitude. In addition, Gouldner (1961) suggests that humans accept the norm of reciprocity and feel a constraint to reward those who have rewarded them. Carrying this line of thought a bit further, it might be argued that a group member who finds group interaction providing good outcomes for him- or herself feels a "vested interest" in maintaining the group as an entity. Such vested interest in the group may lead one to wish to contribute to good reward-cost outcomes for the other group member(s) in order to help insure the continuance of the group and the pattern(s) of interaction within it which provide good reward-cost outcomes for oneself. Thus, there are several reasons for thinking that competent role enactment on the part of one group member is likely to be reciprocated by such performance by other group members. Some data bearing on this proposition will be presented.

Proposition 5, stating that individuals who receive good reward-cost outcomes from their spouses are likely to be satisfied with their marriages, draws on both Homans' principle of distributive justice and Thibaut and Kelley's concept of comparison level. The latter proposes that each individual has a ratio of costs to rewards in any situation which provides outcomes he or she feels are deserved and should be received. If one receives outcomes at or above that level, one is satisfied with one's relationship with that individual or individuals. In applying this principle to a family with its several disparate roles, he (she) will be better satisfied the more roles in which his (her) spouse performs at or above the comparison level.

With respect to Proposition 6, Thibaut and Kelley's comparison level for alternatives provides appropriate conceptualization. One leaves a group or terminates interaction with a specific individual when better reward-cost outcomes are available. The more one is rewarded through the role enactment of a spouse, the better one's reward-cost outcomes are likely to be, and the less likely that the alternative of single status or of an alternative spouse could be expected to provide better reward-costs outcomes. Therefore, the more competent the role performance of one or both spouses, the less likely the marital dissolution. We shall test this proposition only indirectly, since we have no divorce data.

THE INDICATORS

Each respondent was asked to estimate his or her own competence in each family role. In addition, they were asked to estimate the competence of their spouse (described and illustrated in Chapter 2). This latter indicator of *the perceived competence of the spouse* is the measure used in the present analysis.

Wording paralleling the following example (the therapeutic role) was used for each role:

"How well do you feel you do at helping your husband with his personal problems? How well do you feel your husband does at helping you with your personal problems?" Responses provided were: (1) extremely well, (2) quite well, (3) fairly well, (4) rather poorly, (5) extremely poorly, and (6) doesn't try. The last response was excluded from the analysis.

Two indicators of marital happiness were included in the study: whether if one had to do it over, he or she would marry or remain single; the other, whether he or she would prefer to marry the same person. Only the latter item was utilized in the present analysis. Its wording was:

"If you were to marry again, would you want to marry the same person?" The response categories were: (1) yes, certainly, (2) yes, probably, (3) entirely undecided, (4) no, probably, and (5) no, certainly.

Data were obtained on role competence of husbands and wives as reported by their spouses for both sexes for the child care, child socialization, recreational, and therapeutic roles. An indirect measure of competence in the sexual role was employed; namely, the amount of satisfaction that the wife experienced from sexual intercourse with her spouse. If she reported the sexual experience was always or usually intensely gratifying, this was taken as evidence of the sexual role competence of the husband.[1] In addition, data on the competence of the husband (only) in the provider and the wife (only) in the housekeeper role was obtained and employed in the following analysis.[2]

All cases with missing data were eliminated as were those who responded with "don't do it" or "don't try." After these were eliminated, the N for males was 179, for females, 184.

FINDINGS

The research hypothesis was stated as follows: *The greater the role competence of a role player (as reported by his [her] spouse), the greater the marital satisfaction of the role enactor's spouse.* Put slightly differently, persons whose spouses are more competent role enactors are more likely to be better satisfied with their marriages. This research hypothesis most directly tests number 5 of the propositions derived from social exchange and stated above, which states, "Individuals (and couples) who receive good reward-cost outcomes from each other are likely to be satisfied with their marriages." However, support for the research hypothesis would also provide strong indirect support for the other propositions listed.

The initial test of the research hypothesis is provided by a multiple regression analysis relating competence by the husband in six roles to the marital satisfaction of the wife; of the competence of the wife in five roles to the marital satisfaction of the husband. This analysis is summarized in Figures 11.1 and 11.2.

Although issue may be taken with the interval-level measurement assumption made in the application of multiple regression procedures to these data, the authors feel that any analytical errors that may result are more than outweighed by the advantages of the powerful regression procedures.

The six role competence items account for 36.0 percent of the variance in the wives' marital satisfaction scores, but these minus the sexual role account for 9.1 percent of the variance in the husbands' scores. It appears that the role competence of husbands (within the family roles measured) is more important to wives than the role competence of wives to husbands.

The relationship between perceived role competence and marital satisfaction demonstrated in Figures 11.1 and 11.2 may be subject to the criticism that other structural variables such as socioeconomic status, the number of children, or the number of years married may be correlated with both role competence and marital satisfaction. In order to examine the possibility of spurious relationships, thirteen structural variables were measured to control for their effect on the relationship between role competence and marital satisfaction. The variables included were:

(1) husband's occupational prestige

(2) wife's employment status

(3) total family income

(4) husband's education

(5) wife's education

(6) religious affiliation differences

(7) husband's age at marriage

(8) wife's age at marriage

(9) husband's marital status

(10) wife's marital status

(11) age differences

(12) number of years married

(13) number of children

If these thirteen variables are entered into the multiple regression equations along with the role competence variables, the computation of a multiple partial correlation coefficient can provide an indication of the amount of variance in marital satisfaction that is explained by the role competence variables after the effect of the thirteen social variables has been removed. For a discussion and illustration of this procedure, see Blalock (1960). It might be argued that this procedure is unnecessary, since our interest is in role competence and we are not, at this time, concerned about its antecedents; however, if role competence is correlated with social class, length of marriage, and other social variables, it is possible that other valued or devalued properties of individuals and their behavior might influence marital satisfaction independently of role enactment. Controlling for the above thirteen items, the squared multiple partial correlation coefficient for the six roles enacted by the husband is .372 for the wife's marital satisfaction, and .139 for the correlation of the competence of the wife in five roles on the marital satisfaction of the husband. It appears, therefore, that the variance associated with role performance cannot be explained by the usual social background variables.[3]

Some roles predict marital satisfaction much better than others (Figures 11.1 and 11.2). For both husbands and wives, effectiveness in the therapeutic role is the best predictor of male and female satisfaction with the marriage. Competence in child socialization also predicts male and female marital satisfaction about equally for both sexes. Other data from this study show that child socialization is a role in which both parents experience many doubts concerning their own adequacy. Strain relevant to this role

Figure 11.1

THE HUSBAND'S MODEL*

The Husband's Evaluation of
the Wife's Competence in
Each of the Following Roles:

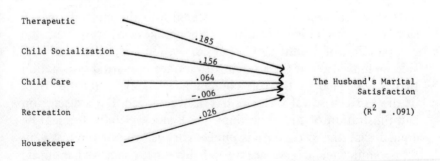

*The values in this figure are normalized regression coefficients (Beta weights) from the multiple regression equation in which marital satisfaction is the dependent variable and the role competence items are independent variables. The values represent the fraction of the change in standard deviations of marital satisfaction attributable to each of the role competence items when all other independent variables are held constant.

Figure 11.2

THE WIFE'S MODEL*

The Wife's Evaluation of
the Husband's Competence in
Each of The Following Roles:

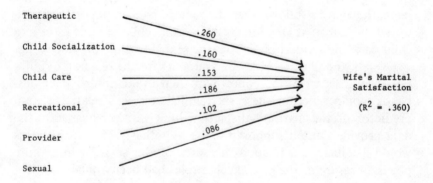

Therapeutic

Child Socialization

Child Care

Recreational

Provider

Sexual

.260
.160
.153
.186
.102
.086

Wife's Marital
Satisfaction

$(R^2 = .360)$

*The values in this figure are normalized regression coefficients (Beta weights) from the multiple regression equation in which marital satisfaction is the dependent variable and the role competence items are independent variables. The values represent the fraction of the change in standard deviations of marital satisfaction attributable to each of the role competence items when all other independent variables are held constant.

may lead to a comparatively high value on the spouse's competence in the role.

The other roles have quite different relationships to marital satisfaction. For wives, the husbands' competence in the recreational role predicts satisfaction as well as does the child socialization role but wives' competence in it has no value for predicting satisfaction of the husbands. It might be remembered that these women have one or more young children at home. They may be grateful to have a man competent in organizing materials and schedules for recreation outside of the home. Variance in female competence in the recreational and child care roles shows no or only trivial predictive value, and the housekeeper role is only of modest value in predicting the marital satisfaction of the male. As noted earlier, we did not have a viable measure of female sexual competence available at the time these data were gathered. Previous research would lead us to expect some predictive value for such competence.

While only two of the roles contribute substantially, and a third modestly to predicting the marital satisfaction of the husband, the competence of the husband in all the family roles contributes to the prediction of the satisfaction of the wife. Competence in the recreational role follows the therapeutic role in importance, followed by substantial contributions from child socialization and child care and modest ones from the sexual and the provider roles.

Overall, the data provide solid support for the research hypothesis insofar as wives are concerned—their evaluation of their husbands' competence in these six familial roles is a relatively good predictor of the marital satisfaction of wives. For husbands, the data provide limited support for the hypothesis. Presumably, this would be increased if good measures of the sexual and a more precise measure of the housekeeper roles had been available.

RECIPROCAL REWARDS THROUGH ROLE ENACTMENT

We have suggested (proposition 4) that individuals who provide good reward-cost outcomes for other group members are more likely to receive good outcomes in turn. If this is true, then a spouse receiving high rewards from the spouse as a product of his (her) role competence should reciprocate with superior role performance in return. To test this proposition, the role competence of the husband (as reported by the wife) is correlated with the role competence of the wife (as reported by the husband) (see Table 11.1).

The data are generally supportive of the proposition. However, many of the correlations in Table 11.1 are statistically nonsignificant. While consistent with the notion of reciprocity in role performance, the data do not provide exceptional support and would also be congruent with a selective proposition: that competent women tend to marry competent men.

Table 11.1.

CORRELATIONS BETWEEN THE ROLE EFFECTIVENESS SCORES OF HUSBANDS AND WIVES

Wives' Effectiveness Scores	Child Care	Child Soc.	Sexual	Recreational	Therapeutic	Provider
			Husbands' Effectiveness Scores			
Child Care	.268	.150	.031	.076	.036	.281
Child Socialization	.285	.250	.156	.180	.170	.273
Recreational	.147	.122	.193	.248	.139	.114
Therapeutic	.109	.024	.238	.267	.262	.143
Housekeeper	.199	.238	.032	.310	.179	.099

OTHER VARIANCE IN MARITAL SATISFACTION

UNDEVELOPED POTENTIAL IN REWARDING BEHAVIOR

It may be possible to improve prediction from role competence by two variations in the measures presently employed. One of these, an adequate indicator of sexual competence, has already been mentioned. Second, we did not ask for an evaluation of the husband in the housekeeper role or the wife in the provider role. These may well have some potential for explaining marital satisfaction. Also, some rewarding behavior may not be measurable through role competence. For example, being a pleasant, cheerful person may be rewarding, and such properties as that may not be taken into account by the respondent in reacting to any of the role measures.

DIFFERENTIAL COSTS FROM SPOUSE

Present data are limited to rewards. However, any group exacts costs from its members in terms of responsibilities required and autonomy foregone. A closely knit multi-bonded group such as the family is likely to be a high-cost group. We suggest that loss of autonomy may be a crucial variable in assessing total spousal costs and goodness of outcomes in the marriage. Some people attempt to maintain constant control over the spouse with a continuous stream of commands, complaints, and suggestions. Thus, a spouse who has certain family-related role responsibilities may find that he (she) has to contend with the attempts of the spouse to specify how, when, and with whom they are performed. The "back seat driver" is a familiar example of attempts to deprive the role enactor of autonomy.

Another variable is in the degree of exclusiveness of the spousal relationship. Some are unwilling for the spouse to travel, have friends not shared with the spouse, or for one to take part in recreation without the other. Such limiting practices reduce individual autonomy greatly.

Finally, the failure of a spouse to enact a familial role at an acceptable level may lead to the spouse doing his (her) work as well as her (his) own, or it may require that a non-family member be hired to perform the responsibilities the spouse is unwilling or unable to perform. Either increases costs to the spouse. These are presumably only a few of numerous differential costs which spouses exact. A more comprehensive list adequately operationalized might greatly increase the proportion of explained variance in satisfaction with marriage and provide a more complete test of social exchange theory.

DISCUSSION

The research hypothesis tested stated, "The greater the role competence of the role player, the more likely a high level of marital satisfaction of the role enactor's spouse."

Competence of wives in two of the roles are far more useful than the others: therapeutic and child socialization. We are not surprised that the therapeutic role is important. Men live in a complex, changing, and often insecure environment where the interpretation of meanings is often difficult and the outcomes of alternative actions are obscure. To have a ready source of help in dealing with this milieu should be important, and the data suggest that it is. Child socialization is a particularly difficult role for parents as children get older. Parents feel unlimited responsibilities for their children without sufficient knowledge and/or authority to carry these responsibilities effectively (LeMasters, 1974: ch. 1). It is not surprising that a wife capable in this role would be valued.

Child care is a simpler role with which mothers have few anxieties. The housekeeper role has been declining in importance, as more of its tasks are performed by outside agencies. Recreation is important to husbands, but apparently the abilities of wives to organize and get it started is not valued.

Steven McLaughlin has suggested that it is the roles involving "companionship" such as the therapeutic and recreational that provide the greatest rewards for the wife. In addition, it is the husband's competence in roles often left entirely to the wife, such as the child care and child socialization roles, that are perceived as rewarding by the wife. In contrast, wives may take the provider and sexual roles of men "for granted."

Returning to the propositions derived from social exchange

(above), the test of the research hypothesis provides some support for all of them but more directly for some than for others. Support is perhaps obvious for propositions 1, 2, 3, and 5. Support for proposition 6 is necessarily indirect since no marital dissolution data are available. Support for it rests on the close relationship, well established empirically, between marital dissatisfaction and marital dissolution. The data are congruent with proposition 4, but they are also compatible with the alternative proposition that effective persons marry effective spouses.

In the introductory section of this paper, we explored the possibility that the high rewards resulting from competent role enactment might be accompanied by high costs (even equally high costs) in terms of high expectations for reciprocal role enactment by the role player's spouse, by less autonomy accorded by spouse or other unspecified costs. The positive coefficients between role enactment and marital satisfactions provide evidence against such notions and support the proposition that the higher rewards resulting from competent role enactment are likely to be accompanied by better outcomes (or higher profits) for other group members.

FURTHER RESEARCH

The present paper constitutes a limited development of the potential in social exchange theory for the study of marital interaction. In order to develop this potential more fully, some of the following might be undertaken:

(1) Develop a more effective indicator of sexual competence for both sexes and extend present measurement to include men in the housekeeper role and women in the provider role.

(2) Develop additional concepts of rewards supplied by one spouse to the other. These might include (without being limited to) the following: (a) certain rewarding aspects of personality not directly involved in role performance, and (b) rewarding behavior or attributes favorable to transactions beyond the family group (in addition to those measured in the provider role).

(3) Develop concepts and indicators to measure differential costs experienced by a person in interaction with and as a consequence of being married to his (her) spouse.

(4) Extend items 2 and 3 above to include interaction with children and/or other members of the household, and perhaps to the spouse's kin outside the household, to the extent that the couple is in interaction with them.

(5) Weight roles by perceived importance.

The greater utility of role competence in predicting female than male marital satisfaction (if it should be validated by further research) has implications for the general nature of marriage. Bernard (1973) states that in any given couple there are two marriages: one as experienced by the wife and one as by the husband. These data give credence to her statement. They also provide still more documentation for the necessity of gathering family normative, value and behavioral data from *both* men and women.

NOTES

1. This is not, in our estimation, an adequate indicator of sexual competence. Even so, the corresponding information was not available for the husband's satisfaction with the wife's performance. Through an oversight, that item was asked only of the wife's perception of her husband's satisfaction with his sexual experience. There is no correlation between her perception of her husband's sexual satisfaction and his report of his satisfaction with the marriage. This lack of a viable indicator constitutes one of the limitations of the present analysis.

2. Through an error, the husband was not asked to evaluate his wife's competence in the housekeeper role. The best estimate available in these data is the wife's self-evaluation of her own competence in the role, which is employed here.

3. Some of these social variables *are* correlated with marital satisfaction independent of measures of role competence, but it is additional variance rather than that explained by role competence.

POSTSCRIPT: TOWARD FURTHER RESEARCH

This volume describes a large initial study of family roles—one designed to develop, sharpen, and refine role concepts, to develop and test empirical indicators of these concepts, and to provide some initial data concerning role behavior of one category of families—those with pre-adolescent children. We have attempted a role delineation which is relatively specific and concrete, which could be empirically measured and utilized to record the various dimensions of role from role norms to role strain.

At this point, we feel the delineation has enjoyed a measure of success. However, we are aware of at least one substantive limitation. It involves the responsibilities involved in the repair and maintenance of the family dwelling and of the yard or other surrounding areas. These responsibilities and behaviors do not logically fit into any of the eight familial roles conceptualized, yet do not seem to have comparable generality and significance warranting conceptualization as a ninth role. This arena of family behavior remains residual to the present conceptualization.

In this initial process, a few ideas were tried and dropped, either as having very limited utility or as useful only for certain purposes. The former includes the concept of role value. We found relatively little variation in the value accorded the eight areas. If a set of responsibilities is viewed as the duty of occupants of one or more positions, and if sanctions are provided for enforcement, the behavior must be highly valued by most. In addition, if one wishes a comparative value, it may be implied from the severity of sanctions respondents would impose for nonperformance of the role. The concept of "task" illustrates the second situation—of a concept useful in limited circumstances. It is useful to explore and measure the normative prescriptions within a role, but it is space- and time-consuming, and it cannot deal with role proscriptions, because a task is a positive concept. In the detailed study of a single role, it could be utilized to provide structure for detailed prescriptions, but it would have to be supplemented with normative proscriptions of similar detail.

This initial study has posed many questions which we have not, to date, pursued, assuming that refined analyses will be more profitable with larger and more diverse samples. For example, women with larger families are more likely to report strain in the kinship role. However, such families also have lower incomes and are older (completed families). Is it family size per se, limited incomes, or the stage in the family life cycle which is the relevant variable? Insofar as substantive issues are concerned, the initial study has raised many research issues and reached few final conclusions. While one might argue that that is the expected situation in social science research, additional studies with larger and more diverse samples will bring many issues nearer closure.

As a result of the initial study described here, the instruments developed for husbands and wives have been shortened and combined into a single instrument, which can be completed by either sex. The revised instrument has been published as Technical Bulletin 82, "Role Structure and Analysis of the Family: The Washington Family Role Inventory," Agricultural Research Center, Washington State University, Pullman, Washington.

As we see it, the *initial* conceptual and measurement tasks have been completed, but the larger task of measuring and analyzing family role structure and behavior is only started. Comparative studies of family roles are needed between the major regions of the United States. We are convinced that there are major differences between the family in the West, the South, and the Midwest; among the major ethnic and racial groups in the society and between the social classes. Eventually, cross-cultural research would be extremely useful. Too, comparative studies along the family life cycle, in partial or attenuated families, and studies of role transitions as individuals move from married to single statuses and back again into married status could provide much more insight into those segments of family life.

The need that fathered (or mothered, if you like) this study was the feeling that family research had been too fragmentary to provide any accurate or adequate description of American family norms and behavior. Sound theory development and testing must be based on accurate and reasonably adequate information about the family. This need for a national study of the family still exists; in fact, it has become more urgent because of the increased tempo of change in the family and the diversity of assertions about its structure and behavior which have appeared in the first half of the decade of the 1970s. Such a national study should be based on a probability sample of American families utilizing an interview technique to obtain as complete a sample as possible.

Finally, we are interested in family role studies as social "bench marks." To date, statements about the changing structure and behavior patterns of the family have had to be either extremely limited or intuitive for lack of specific data gathered systematically over time from an identifiable population. Repeated studies of role structure, enactment, and psychological properties with samples from the same population would go far toward providing accurate and conceptually significant measures of the nature and extent of family change in a society.

—F.I.N.

REFERENCES

ADAMS, BERT N. (1970) "Isolation, function, and beyond: American kinship in the 1960s." Journal of Marriage and the Family 32 (November): 575-597.
——— (1968) Kinship in an Urban Setting. Chicago: Markham.
ALDOUS, JOAN (1969) "Occupational characteristics and males: role performance in the family." Journal of Marriage and the Family 31 (November): 707-713.
ARENDT, HANNAH (1959) The Human Condition. Garden City, N.Y.: Doubleday.
ARNOTT, C. C. (1972) "Married women and the pursuit of profit: an exchange theory perspective." Journal of Marriage and the Family 34 (February): 122-134.

BAHR, STEPHEN JOSEPH (1972) "A methodological study of conjugal power: a replication and extension of Blood and Wolfe." Ph.D. dissertation. Washington State University.
BANTON, MICHAEL (1965) Roles. New York: Basic Books.
BARTZ, K. B. and F. IVAN NYE (1970) "Early marriage: a propositional formulation." Journal of Marriage and the Family 32 (May).
BATES, FREDERICK L. (1956) "Position, role and status: a reformulation of concepts." Social Forces 34 (May): 313-321.
BELL, RICHARD Q. (1968) "A reinterpretation of the direction of effects in studies of socialization." Psychological Review 75: 81-95.
BELL, ROBERT (1971) "Female sexual satisfaction as related to levels of education." Sexual Behavior (November): 8-15.
BERARDO, FELIX M. (1967) "Kinship interaction and communications among space-age migrants." Journal of Marriage and the Family 29 (August): 541-554.

――― (1966) "Kinship interaction and migrant adaptation in an aerospace-related community." Journal of Marriage and the Family 28 (August): 296-304.

BERNARD, JESSIE (1973) "My four revolutions: an autobiographical history of the ASA." American Journal of Sociology 78 (January): 773-791.

――― (1972) "Women, marriage, and the future." Futurist 4 (April): 41-43.

BIDDLE, B. J. and E. J. THOMAS (1966) Role Theory: Concepts and Research. New York: John Wiley.

BINSTOCK, JEANNE (1972) "Motherhood, an occupation facing decline." Futurist 6 (June): 99-102.

BLALOCK, HUBERT M., Jr. (1960) Social Statistics, New York: McGraw-Hill.

BLAU, PETER, M. (1964) Exchange and Power in Social Life. New York: John Wiley.

BLOOD, ROBERT O., Jr. (1964) "Impact of urbanization on American family structure and functioning." Sociology and Social Research 49 (October).

――― and DONALD M. WOLFE (1960) Husbands and Wives: The Dynamics of Married Living. New York: Free Press.

BOTT, ELIZABETH (1957) Family and Social Network. London: Tavistock.

BRIM, O. G. (1959) Education for Child Rearing. New York: Russell Sage.

BRONFENBRENNER, URIE (1970) Two Worlds of Childhood. New York: Russell Sage.

――― (1958) "Socialization and social class through time and space," in E. E. Maccoby et al. (eds.) Readings in Social Psychology. New York: Holt, Rinehart & Winston.

BURCH, WILLIAM (1969) "The social circles of leisure: competing explanations." Journal of Leisure Research 1: 125-145.

――― (1966) "Wilderness—The life cycle and forest recreational choice." Journal of Forestry 64: 606-610.

――― (1965) "The play world of camping: research into the social meaning of outdoor recreation." American Journal of Sociology 70: 604-612.

――― (1964a) "Nature as symbol and expression in American social life." Ph.D. dissertation. University of Minnesota.

――― (1964b) "Two concepts for guiding recreation management decisions." Journal of Forestry 62: 707-712.

――― and MARVIN TAVES (1961) "Changing functions of recreation in human society: outdoor recreation in the Upper Great Lakes area." Lake States Forest Experiment Station, Station Paper 89: 8-16.

BURDGE, R. (1969) "Levels of occupational prestige and leisure activity." Journal of Leisure Research 1: 363-373.

――― (1965) "Selected occupational influences on the use of outdoor recreation." Presented at the Rural Sociological Society meeting, Chicago, Illinois. (mimeo)

BURGESS, ERNEST W. and PAUL WALLIN (1953) Engagement and Marriage. Philadelphia: J. B. Lippincott.

――― and LEONARD S. COTTRELL (1939) Predicting Success or Failure in Marriage. Englewood Cliffs, N.J.: Prentice-Hall.

BURR, WESLEY R. (1973) Theory Construction and the Sociology of the Family. New York: John Wiley.

CAMPBELL, FREDERICK L. (1970) "Family growth and variation in family role structure." Journal of Marriage and the Family 32: 45-53.

CARLSON, JOHN EDWARD (1972) "A sociological analysis of factors affecting recreation behavior." Ph.D. dissertation, Washington State University.

CLARK, ALEXANDER L. and PAUL WALLIN (1965) "Women's sexual responsiveness and the duration and quality of their marriages." American Journal of Sociology 71: 187-196.

--- and PAUL WALLIN (1964) "The accuracy of husbands' and wives' reports on the frequency of marital coitus." Population Studies 18: 165-173.

CLARKE, ALFRED C. (1956) "The use of leisure and its relation to levels of occupational prestige." American Sociological Review 21: 301-307.

CLAWSON, MARION (1964) "How much leisure, now and in the future?" in James Charlesworth (ed.) Leisure in America: Blessing or Curse? Philadelphia: American Academy of Political and Social Science Monograph 4: 1-20.

CONNOR, RUTH, THEODORE B. JOHANNIS, Jr., and JAMES WALTERS (1955) "Family recreation in relation to role conceptions of family members." Marriage and Family Living 17: 306-309.

CUNNINGHAM, KENNETH R. and THEODORE B. JOHANNIS, Jr. (1960) "Research on family and leisure: a review and critique of selected studies." Family Life Coordinator 9: 25-32.

DAVIS, H. (1970) "Technological change and recreation planning," in B. L. Driver (ed.) Elements of Outdoor Recreation Planning. Ann Arbor, Mich.: University Microfilms: 113-120.

DE GRAZIA, SEBASTIAN (1962) Of Time, Work, and Leisure. New York: Twentieth Century Fund.

DENTLER, ROBERT and PETER PINEO (1960) "Sexual adjustment and personal growth of husbands: a panel analysis." Marriage and Family Living 22: 45-48.

DEVOR, GERALDINE M. (1970) "Children as agents in socializing parents." Family Coordinator 19: 208-212.

DUMAZEDIER, JAFFRE (1967) Toward a Society of Leisure. (Translated from the French by Stewart E. McClure.) New York: Free Press.

EDWARDS, J. and M. BRAUBURGER (1973) "Exchange and parent-youth conflict." Journal of Marriage and the Family 36 (February): 101-108.

--- (1969) "Familial behavior as social exchange." Journal of Marriage and the Family 31 (August): 518-527.

EKEH, P. (1974) Social Exchange Theory. Cambridge, Mass.: Harvard University Press.

ELLIS, ALBERT (1954) "Female sexual responses and marital relations." Social Problems 1 (April): 152-154.

FARBER, B. (1964) Family Organization and Interaction. San Francisco: Chandler.

FOOTE, NELSON (1957) "Sex as play." Social Problems 1 (April): 159-163.

GEBHARD, PAUL (1966) "Factors in marital orgasm." Journal of Social Issues 22: 90.

GECAS, VIKTOR (1973) "Self-conceptions of migrant and settled Mexican-Americans." Social Science Quarterly 54 (December): 579-594.

GERSON, W. M. (1960) "Leisure and marital satisfaction of college married couples." Marriage and Family Living 22: 360-361.

GIBBS, JACK P. (1965) "Norms: the problem of definition and clarification." American Journal of Sociology 70 (March): 586-594.

GOODE, WILLIAM (1971) "Force and violence in the family." Journal of Marriage and the Family 33 (November).

--- (1963) Family and World Revolution. New York: Free Press.

--- (1960) "A theory of role strain." American Sociological Review 25: 483-496.

--- (1959) "The sociology of the family," pp. 178-196 in Robert K. Merton et al. (eds.) Sociology Today: New York: Basic Books.

--- E. HOPKINS, and H. McCLURE (1971) Social Systems and Family Patterns: A Propositional Inventory. Indianapolis: Bobbs-Merrill.

GOULDNER, ALVIN W. (1961) "The norm of reciprocity." American Sociological Review 25: 161-178.

GREEN, ARNOLD W. (1960) "The middle-class male child and neurosis," in Norman W. Bell and Ezra F. Vogel (eds.) A Modern Introduction to the Family. New York: Free Press.

GROSS, NEAL A., WARD S. MASON and ALEXANDER W. McEACHERN (1958) Explorations in Role Analysis. New York: John Wiley.

GURIN, GERALD, JOSEPH VEROFF and SHEILA FELD (1960) Americans View Their Mental Health. New York: Basic Books.

HACKER, HELEN (1957) "The new burdens of masculinity." Marriage and Family Living 19 (August): 227-234.

HARRY, JOSEPH (1970) "Family localism and social participation." American Journal of Sociology 75: 821-827.

HARTLEY, RUTH E. (1969) "Some implications of current changes in sex-role patterns," in John N. Edwards (ed.) The Family and Change. New York: Alfred A. Knopf.

HEER, DAVID M. (1963) "The measurement and bases of family power: an overview." Marriage and Family Living 25 (May): 133-139.

HEISS, JEROLD (1968) Family Roles and Interaction. Chicago. Rand McNally.

HESS, H. (1970) "Ethnology and developmental psychology," in P. Mussen (ed.) Carmichael's Manual of Child Psychology. New York: John Wiley.

HICKS, MARY W. and MARILYN PLATT (1970) "Marital happiness and stability: a review of the research in the sixties." Journal of Marriage and the Family 32 (November): 553-574.

HILL, REUBEN and ROY H. RODGERS (1964) "The developmental approach," pp. 171-214 in Harold Christensen (ed.) Handbook of Marriage and the Family. Chicago: Rand McNally.

HOFFMAN, LOIS W. and F. IVAN NYE (1974) Working Mothers: Consequences for Men, Women, and Children. San Francisco: Jossey-Bass.

HOMANS, G. (1974) Social Behavior: Its Elementary Forms. New York: Harcourt Brace Jovanovich.

——— (1961) Social Behavior: Its Elementary Forms. New York: Harcourt Brace World.

JACKSON, JAY (1972) Role. London: Cambridge University Press.

JACKSON, JAY (1966) "A conceptual and measurement model for norms and roles." Pacific Sociological Review 9 (Spring): 35-47.

KERCKHOFF, ALAN C. (1972) Socialization and Social Class. Englewood Cliffs, N.J.: Prentice-Hall.

KING, DAVID (1968) "Socio-economic variables related to campsite use." Forest Science 14: 45-54.

KINSEY, ALFRED, WARDWELL POMEROY and CLYDE MARTIN (1948) Sexual Behavior in the Human Male. Philadephia: W. B. Saunders.

——— and PAUL GEBHARD (1953) Sexual Behavior in the Human Female. Philadelphia: W. B. Saunders.

KIRKPATRICK, CLIFFORD (1963) The Family as Process and Institution. New York: Ronald Press.

KOHN, M. (1969) Class and Conformity. Homewood, Ill.: Dorsey.
——— (1963) "Social class and parent-child relationships: an interpretation." American Journal of Sociology 68 (January): 471-480.
KOMAROVSKY, MIRRA (1962) Blue Collar Marriage. New York: Random House
LEICHTER, HOPE JENSEN and WILLIAM E. MITCHELL (1967) Kinship and Casework. New York: Russell Sage.
LE MASTERS, E. E. (1974) Parenthood in Modern America. Homewood, Ill.: Dorsey.
LEVINGER, GEORGE (1966) "Sources of marital dissatisfaction among applicants for divorce." American Journal of Orthopsychiatry 36: 803-807.
——— (1964) "Task and social behavior in marriage." Sociometry 27 (December): 433-448.
LEWIS, LIONEL S. and DENNIS BRISSETT (1967) "Sex as work: a study of avocational counseling." Social Problems 15 (Summer): 8-18.
LINTON, RALPH (1945) The Cultural Background of Personality. New York: Appleton-Century-Crofts.
——— (1936) The Study of Man. New York: Appleton-Century-Crofts.
LITWAK, EUGENE and JOSEFINA FIGUEIRA (1970) "Technological innovation and ideal forms of family structure in an industrial democratic society," in Reuben Hill and Rene Konig (eds.) Family East and West. Paris: Mouton.
LITWAK, EUGENE and IVAN SZELENYI (1969) "Primary group structures and their functions: kin, neighbors, and friends." American Sociological Review 34 (August): 465-481.
LOPATA, HELENA Z. (1971) Occupation: Housewife. New York: Oxford University Press.
——— (1966) "The life cycle of the social role of the housewife." Sociology and Social Research 51 (October): 5-22.
LYNN, DAVID B. (1969) Parental and Sex Role Identification. Berkeley, Calif.: McCutchen.

MASTERS, WILLIAM and VIRGINIA JOHNSON (1970) Human Sexual Inadequacy. Boston: Little, Brown.
——— (1966) Human Sexual Response. Boston: Little, Brown.
MEAD, GEORGE H. (1934) Mind, Self and Society. Chicago: University of Chicago Press.
MERTON, ROBERT K. (1957) Social Theory and Social Structure. New York: The Free Press.
MOWRER, HARRIET (1954) "Sex and marital adjustment: a critique of Kinsey's approach." Social Problems 1 (April): 147-152.

NYE, F. IVAN (1974) "Emerging and declining roles." Journal of Marriage and the Family 36 (May): 238-245.
——— (1958) "Employment status and recreational behavior of mothers." Pacific Sociological Review 1 (Fall): 69-72.
——— and FELIX M. BERARDO (1973) The Family: Its Structure and Interaction. New York: Macmillan.
NYE, F. IVAN and LOIS HOFFMAN (1963) The Employed Mother in America. Chicago: Rand McNally.
NYE, F. IVAN and EVELYN MAC DOUGAL (1959) "Do families have subcultures?" Sociology and Social Research 44 (May-June): 311-316.

NYE, F. IVAN, JOHN CARLSON and GERALD GARRETT (1970) "Family size, interaction, affect and stress." Journal of Marriage and the Family 32 (May).

NYE, F. IVAN, LYNN WHITE and JAMES FRIDERES (1973) "Role competence and marital dissolution." International Journal of Sociology of the Family 3 (March).

OGBURN, WILLIAM F. (1938) "The changing family." Family 19 (July): 139-143.

ORDEN, S. R. and N. M. BRADBURN (1968) "Dimensions of marital happiness." American Journal of Sociology (May): 715-731.

OSOFSKY, JOY D. (1970) "The shaping of mother's behavior by children." Journal of Marriage and the Family 32 (August): 400-405.

PARSONS, TALCOTT and ROBERT F. BALES (1955) Family, Socialization and Interaction Process. New York: Free Press.

PINEO, PETER (1961) "Disenchantment in later years of marriage." Marriage and Family Living 23 (February): 3-12.

RAINWATER, LEE (1965) Family Design: Marital Sexuality, Family Size, and Contraception. Chicago: Aldine.

REISS, I. (1965) "The universality of the family: a conceptual analysis." Journal of Marriage and the Family 27 (November): 443-453.

REISS, PAUL J. (1962) "The extended kinship system: correlates of and attitudes on frequency of interaction." Marriage and Family Living 24 (November): 333-339.

RHEINGOLD, HARRIET L. (1969) "The social and socializing infant," pp. 779-790 in David Goslin (ed.) Handbook of Socialization Theory and Research. Chicago: Rand McNally.

RICHER, STEPHEN (1968) "The economics of child rearing." Journal of Marriage and the Family 30 (August): 462-466.

ROBINS, LEE N. and MIRODA TOMANEC (1962) "Closeness to blood relatives outside the immediate family." Marriage and Family Living 24 (November): 340-346.

RODMAN, HYMAN (1972) "Marital power: the theory of resources in cultural context." Journal of Comparative Family Studies 3 (Spring): 50-69.

ROSSI, ALICE S. (1968) "Transition to parenthood." Journal of Marriage and the Family 30: 26-39.

SAFILIOS-ROTHSCHILD, CONSTANTINA (1970) "The study of family power structure: a review 1960-1969." Journal of Marriage and the Family 32 (November): 539-552.

SCANZONI, JOHN H. (1972) Sexual Bargaining: Power Politics in the American Marriage. Englewood Cliffs, N.J.: Prentice-Hall.

SIMPSON, R. L. (1972) Theories of Social Exchange. Morristown, N.J.: General Learning Press.

SMITH, ROBERT B. (1972) "Neighborhood context and college plans: an ordinal path analysis." Social Forces 51 (December): 199-217.

SPOCK, BENJAMIN (1957) The Common Sense Book of Baby and Child Care. New York: Sloan & Pearce.

SUSSMAN, MARVIN B. and LEE G. BURCHINAL (1962) "Kin family network: unheralded structure in current conceptualizations of family functioning." Journal of Marriage and the Family 24 (August): 231-240.

SWINEHART, JAMES W. (1963) "Socio-economic level, status aspiration, and maternal role." American Sociological Review 28 (June): 391-399.

TERMAN, L. M. et al. (1938) Psychological Factors in Marital Happiness. New York: McGraw-Hill.

THIBAUT, J. W. and H. H. KELLEY (1959) The Social Psychology of Groups. New Nork: John Wiley.

TURNER, RALPH H. (1970) Family Interaction. New York: John Wiley.

——— (1962) "Some family determinants of ambition." Sociology and Social Research 46 (July): 397-411.

U. S. Bureau of Census (1973) Detailed Characteristics (United States). Washington, D.C.: Government Printing Office.

——— (1972a) The County and City Data Book. Washington, D.C.: Government Printing Office.

——— (1972b) Detailed Characteristics (State of Washington). Washington, D.C.: Government Printing Office.

WALLER, WILLARD and REUBEN HILL (1951) The Family: A Dynamic Interpretation. New York: Holt, Rinehart & Winston.

——— (1938) The Family: A Dynamic Interpretation. New York: Holt, Rinehart & Winston.

——— (1937) "The rating and dating complex." American Sociology Review 2 (October): 727-734.

WALLIN, PAUL (1960) "A study of orgasm as a condition of women's enjoyment of intercourse." Journal of Social Psychology 51: 191-198.

——— and ALEXANDER CLARK (1958a) "Marital satisfaction and husbands' and wives' perception of similarity in their preferred frequency of coitus." Journal of Abnormal and Social Psychology 57: 370-373.

WALLIN, PAUL and ALEXANDER CLARK (1958b) "Cultural norms and husbands' and wives' reports of their marital partners' preferred frequency of coitus relative to their own." Sociometry 21: 247-254.

WEIGERT, ANDREW J. and DARWIN L. THOMAS (1971) "Family as a conditional universal." Journal of Marriage and the Family 33 (February): 188-196.

WEST, PATRICK and L. C. MERRIAM, Jr. (1969) "Camping and cohesiveness: a sociological study of the effect of outdoor recreation on family solidarity." Minnesota Forestry Research Notes 201.

WHYTE, WILLIAM H. (1953) "The wife problem," in Robert F. Winch and Robert McGuinnis (eds.) Selected Studies in Marriage and the Family. New York: Holt, Rinehart & Winston.

WOLFE, DONALD M. (1959) "Power and authority in the family," chapter 7 in D. S. Cartwright (ed.) Studies in Social Power. Ann Arbor, Mich.: Institute for Social Research.

WOLFENSTEIN, MARTHA (1963) "Fun morality: an analysis of recent American child-training literature," chapter 10 in Margaret Mead and Martha Wolfenstein (eds.) Childhood in Contemporary Cultures. Chicago: University of Chicago Press.

YOUNG, MICHAEL and PETER WILLMOTT (1957) Kinship and Family in East London. New York: Free Press.

ZELDITCH, MORRIS, Jr. (1955) "Role differentiation in the nuclear family: a comparative study," chapter 6 in Talcott Parsons and Robert F. Bales, Family socialization and Interaction Process. New York: Free Press.

ZNANIECKI, FLORIAN (1965) Social Relations and Social Role. San Francisco: Chandler.